Living on the Edge

Life at the Montauk Point Lighthouse 1930-1945

Henry Osmers

Outskirts Press, Inc.
Denver, Colorado

Living on the Edge
Life at the Montauk Point Lighthouse 1930-1945

Outskirts Press, Inc.
http://www.outskirtspress.com

ISBN: 978-1-4327-2950-9

Library of Congress Control Number: 2008942984

Outskirts Press and the "OP" logo are trademarks belonging to Outskirts Press, Inc.

PRINTED IN THE UNITED STATES OF AMERICA

In memory of my parents,

Henry Osmers (1918-1983) and Margaret Osmers (1918-1999),
who introduced me to the beauty of Montauk at the right time.

Contents

List of Illustrations

Framed by a window opening in a World War II sentry post, the Montauk Point Lighthouse stands proudly on Turtle Hill, August 2007. (Author Photo)

Preface

In the seven years I have served as a docent at the Montauk Point Lighthouse Museum, I have attempted to learn as much as possible about the history of this famous landmark. The desire became a passion and resulted in the publication of *On Eagle's Beak: A History of the Montauk Point Lighthouse in* 2008. My research revealed the many scientific developments that, over a span of nearly 200 years, moved the lighthouse from whale oil lamps and hand-wound clockworks to electricity and automation. But more importantly, it introduced me to the marvelous and poignant stories of the lighthouse keepers who maintained it.

These men of varying backgrounds and personalities brought their individual talents and skills to Montauk. Some may not have been proficient in many trades, but given the frugal lifestyle of the lonely keeper, they learned out of necessity. Whether the job called for carpentry in repairing a window in the keeper's dwelling or the lighthouse, applying paint to anything that didn't move, or dangling down the side of the tower when applying whitewash, these men strove to keep the light station in a condition worthy of approval by the most critical inspector.

While at the lighthouse one afternoon in June 2007, long time tour guide Audrey Loebl introduced me to a special visitor, a spry, congenial woman named Margaret Buckridge Bock. She was the daughter of Thomas Buckridge, the last civilian keeper at the lighthouse. Imagine my excitement at meeting lighthouse history in the flesh! I escorted her through the museum and asked her to participate in one of my lighthouse history presentations. Visitors were enthralled by her recollection of events and the stories she told of life at the lighthouse in the 1930s. She smiled and chuckled at their surprised responses.

Margaret Buckridge Bock became the inspiration for this book about life at the Montauk Point Lighthouse in the 1930s. An interview with her was arranged, and in early July 2007 my wife, Terri, and I went to see her. In the comfort of her beautiful 1815 home in Westbrook, Connecticut, Margaret Buckridge Bock shared memories of her years at the Montauk Lighthouse and offered me memorabilia for my manuscript. I soon discovered she prefers the nickname of "Bucky" (As she put it: "Anything but Mrs. Bock!"). And so, Bucky is how I refer to her throughout most of this book.

The meeting with Margaret Buckridge Bock was followed in October 2007 by another exciting glimpse into lighthouse history when I had a telephone conversation with Jonathan Miller, son of first assistant keeper Jonathan A. ("Jack") Miller. The senior Miller was stationed at Montauk during the 1930s with Thomas Buckridge.

His son's insights into daily life at the lighthouse and his experience during the Great Hurricane of 1938 were both revealing and thrilling.

Then, in August 2008, I met Sheila Jones while I was working at the top of the lighthouse. She is the daughter of Arthur (Art) Dunne, who was stationed at the Montauk Point Light Station during World War II. We arranged for an interview with her father who lives in Amagansett, about 17 miles from Montauk Point. Days later I met Art and he filled in the blanks about life at the lighthouse during the war, telling me fascinating, exciting, and at times very amusing stories.

The memories of Margaret Buckridge Bock, Jonathan Miller, and Arthur Dunne form the backbone of this book. *Living on the Edge* is intended to give not only a glimpse of Montauk Point Lighthouse during the 1930s and early 1940s, but also a personal look into the lives of the families who lived at the station during that time— the lightkeeping experiences of Thomas Buckridge, Jack Miller, and George Warrington, and the wartime experiences shared by Art Dunne. It is my hope that readers will come away with feelings of wonder and awe about a vanished lifestyle that was lived by so many and now recalled by so few.

Margaret Buckridge Bock visits her childhood home, the Montauk Point Lighthouse, in June 2007. (Author Photo)

Acknowledgements

The foundation for this book was laid through the contributions of Margaret Buckridge ("Bucky") Bock. Her generous support with photos, documents, and first hand accounts is evident throughout this book. Jonathan Miller's perspective of daily chores, interaction with the Coast Guard, and the ordeal of the hurricane of September 21, 1938 enhanced the personal remembrance of life on Montauk. Arthur Dunne's extremely interesting and revealing stories and photographs provided a rich picture of life at the Point during the tumultuous years of World War II.

Brian Pope at the Montauk Point Lighthouse Museum was very helpful and encouraging in the acquisition of certain photos used in this book. Dick White of the Montauk Historical Society provided advice, direction, and encouragement. Special thanks to lighthouse custodian Bob Dippolito, for his kindness and encouragement.

Lighthouse logs were obtained from the National Archives through the help of lighthouse author Candace Clifford. Many documents pertaining to the careers of Thomas Buckridge, Jack Miller, and George Warrington were provided through the National Archives National Personnel Records Center in St. Louis.

As they did with *On Eagle's Beak,* Marci Vail of East Hampton Library's Long Island Collection provided her own brand of encouragement and expertise, and Robin Strong of the Montauk Library provided some beautiful photographs, suggestions, and enlightening wit and wisdom about Montauk history.

Some 1920s Montauk photographs were obtained through the help of the staff of the Long Island Collection at the Queens Borough Public Library in Jamaica, New York: Director James Driscoll, Samantha Dyer, and Eric Huber. Particularly gracious was Judith Todman.

Maria Dennehy of Camera Concepts in Patchogue, Long Island was kind and helpful in formatting two old photographs.

And thanks to those on a personal level: lifelong friend Ron Dutcher for his knowledge and explanation of naval terminology; Bill Yearsley and Edgar Noblesala for their computer wizardry; and finally to Norman Brodsky, who came up with the perfect title for this book after I struggled with the task unsuccessfully for weeks!

Introduction

Montauk
1655-1930s

The Montauk Peninsula encompasses approximately 10,000 acres, located at the east end of Long Island's historic South Fork. The name "Montauk" is derived from its former inhabitants, the Montaukett Indians, once considered the largest and most powerful Indian tribe on Long Island.

The first settlers came to the area in 1655 after Montaukett chief Wyandanch granted permission for an East Hampton group called the Montauk Proprietors to use land for pasturage. In 1660 the Proprietors purchased a section of Montauk for pasturing cattle and sheep and for fishing purposes. Additional land acquisitions in 1670 and 1687 comprise the Montauk we know today.

From 1661 to 1879 the entire peninsula was used for pasturage and fishing by the Proprietors. Three dwellings, First House, Second House, and Third House—all built in the 1740s and later rebuilt—were occupied by keepers, caretakers of the properties who mainly looked after the cattle and sheep. By the mid 1800s all three dwellings had been converted to hotels, taking in visitors who wished to experience the rugged beauty of the Montauk Peninsula. (First House no longer exists, but Second and Third House still stand.)

Perhaps thousands of domesticated animals roamed Long Island at this time. The annual livestock roundup, when vast numbers of cattle and sheep were herded out to Montauk in May and then back home to East Hampton or Amagansett in November, was for many years a major event.

In 1879, Arthur Benson, President of the Brooklyn Union Gas Company and developer of Brooklyn's Bensonhurst section, purchased the entire Montauk Peninsula (except for federal lands at the lighthouse and life saving stations) at auction for $151,000. He intended to turn Montauk into a hunting and fishing resort for several of his wealthy friends. To that end, he created the Montauk Association, a private housing development on the cliffs overlooking the Atlantic Ocean. However, Benson did allow the tradition of pasturage to continue. Benson had other plans for development of Montauk, but they ended with his death in 1889.

Meanwhile, Austin Corbin, president of the Long Island Railroad since 1881, envisioned Montauk as a port of entry for transatlantic steamships and sought to extend the railroad to Montauk, which he accomplished in 1895. There also were plans to develop Montauk in order to accommodate an expected increase in visitors, but the sudden death of Corbin in June of 1896 doomed the project.

During the summer of 1898, Montauk became a quarantine center for about 30,000 troops returning home from the Spanish American War. Some suffered from malaria and yellow fever, and it was believed that Montauk's remote location was well suited for treatment and convalescence. Although the troops were confined at Montauk, they had freedom to ride and take walks. Some visited the lighthouse. Among the troops were Colonel Theodore Roosevelt and his famous Rough Riders. The future President of the United States even found time to visit the lighthouse!

Montauk was again visited by the military during World War I, with the creation of facilities to house dirigibles and a sea plane. Troops and Coast Guard personnel were stationed at a base located at the foot of Fort Pond.

Only a few years after the departure of the military came another attempt at development, but on a more ambitious scale. Carl Fisher, creator of popular Miami Beach, sought to duplicate his Florida feat at Montauk, when he purchased over 5,000 acres in 1925 and later acquired additional properties. To create his "Miami Beach of the North," which included Austin Corbin's dream of a port of entry for ocean liners, Fisher built dozens of miles of roads, opened Lake Montauk to Block Island Sound to create a harbor, built a seven-story office tower in the newly constructed village, and in 1927 completed his majestic centerpiece on Fort Hill—the Montauk Manor. It contained over 170 rooms with numerous luxurious amenities. Fisher also built a yacht club on Star Island. There were tennis courts, polo fields, nurseries for plants and shrubs, and a newly built railroad station.

Meanwhile, New York's master builder, Robert Moses, was busy creating state parks at Hither Hills and Montauk Point. The Montauk Point State Park and the Montauk Manor both opened on May 30, 1927. Such massive developments brought about the end of the time-honored tradition of the cattle drive. No livestock roundup was held after 1925.

Fisher's plans seemed endless and relentless. However, the momentum of development slowed when a major hurricane caused death and destruction at Miami Beach in September 1926, causing Fisher to divert funding and manpower from Montauk to other projects. Serious financial problems plagued his company, and work at Montauk ultimately ceased. He went bankrupt in 1931. Residents of Montauk again heaved a sigh of relief after another attempt to overdevelop their pristine peninsula was averted.

By the 1920s Montauk's reputation as a summer resort was well known. The area also became famous because of "rum-runners" hard at work during the Prohibition Era. Montauk's remote and quiet shores were well suited for boats to deliver their precious contraband cargos of liquor, which then would be transported over land to New York City and elsewhere. A cat and mouse game prevailed between the smugglers and the U.S. Coast Guard, occasionally resulting in gunfire. All the while, certain local residents became wealthy as a result of the illegal activity. These were exciting times, to say the least!

Despite the various businesses, legitimate or otherwise, by 1930, Montauk's population surprisingly was a mere 608 residents. Although the Great Depression of the 1930s brought hardship to many Americans, Montauk continued to be a lively town in many respects. In 1931 the U.S. Navy was using Fort Pond Bay as a base and conducting maneuvers in the Atlantic Ocean. The Montauk Marine Basin opened in 1932, and the next year the Long Island Railroad introduced the "Fisherman's Special," running from Pennsylvania Station in New York City to Montauk. Phineas Dickinson revived the traditional cattle drive in 1936, and opened the Deep Hollow Ranch, which included Third House as a boarding house. The cattle drive lasted until World War II.

MONTAUK PARKWAY AND LIGHTHOUSE - MONTAUK POINT, LONG ISLAND, N. Y.

The end of the road. The "Montauk Parkway" at the lighthouse in 1940. (Courtesy of the Queens Borough Public Library, Long Island Division, Postcard Collection)

auk Point Lighthouse
A Capsule History

; of all types met their doom in the vicinity of Montauk
of New York in the 1600s, and shipping losses increased
t century. Statesman, Revolutionary War patriot and
ommedieu conducted a survey at the point in 1792 and
—being a danger to shipping but also a critical landfall for
of New York. He selected a site atop Turtle Hill for
ouse. President George Washington authorized the
e on April 12th of that year. The 80-foot tall sandstone
McComb, Jr. in 1796 at a cost of $22,300. It went into

e first lightkeeper, selected by the President himself. He
red in 1812. Numerous other keepers followed over the
nd dedicated tradition of safeguarding ships that came
ores. During Henry Baker's time as keeper (1814-1832),
e at Montauk Point and noted their thoughts and special
experiences in the lighthouse's guest register. Keeper Patrick Gould requested an
extension (built 1838) to the existing keeper's dwelling, which proved useful in
accommodating increasing numbers of visitors to the lighthouse. Gould also
distinguished himself as a member of the life saving service at the Point, when on
December 14, 1856 he assisted in the rescue of the crew of the wrecked brig *Flying
Cloud*.

Many changes took place at the light station over the years. Repairs were
made as needed and improvements occurred as technology evolved. In 1806, Josiah
Hand's spider lamp was installed in the lantern, followed by Winslow Lewis'
modified Argand lamp in 1812. Both of these lighting mechanisms produced a
steady, fixed beam of white light. A new lantern was placed atop the lighthouse in
1849.

With the installation of a First Order Fresnel lens on January 1, 1858 the
quality of the light vastly improved. The lens' many prisms captured and focused the
light from an oil lamp and broadcast it some twenty miles at sea in a brilliant beam.
But the light signal's change from a steady beam to a flash every two minutes caused
confusion for a time. There was no way for vessels already at sea to know about the
new signal. To make matters worse, on the same day the flashing Montauk lens was
placed in service, Shinnecock Lighthouse went into operation, 35 miles west at
present-day Hampton Bays, with a steady beam.

Captain Ephraim Harding of the full-rigged sailing ship *John Milton* had no
idea the Montauk Light's signal was altered. His ship had left New York late in 1856,
before the change took place and did not return home for more than a year. As the
John Milton approached Long Island's shores on February 18, 1858, a snowstorm hit
the coast. Captain Harding was able to make out the steady beam of what he
believed to be the Montauk Light, not knowing it was actually the new light at

Shinnecock. He set sail northward toward what he thought was Block Island Sound. At dawn on February 20th the *John Milton* was smashed to pieces on the rocks at Montauk about five miles west of the light. All thirty-three of the crew perished.

The tragedy behind it, the entire light station was renovated in 1860. A new dwelling was built and the height of the tower was raised thirty feet to accommodate additional rooms and the new lens. With a staff of three keepers, beginning in the late 1850s, the Montauk Point Lighthouse was kept in good order for many decades.

Keeper Jonathan A. Miller served two separate terms at Montauk from 1865-1869 and 1872-1875, all with the use of one arm, having lost the other in a Civil War battle. A son, John Ellsworth Miller, later became keeper at Montauk Light.

A fog signal was added to the station in 1873 and a brick fog signal house in 1897. A telephone was installed in 1889 and in 1899 the "daymark", the distinctive brown stripe around the tower's middle, was added. The First Order lens was replaced with a 3½ order bivalve Fresnel lens in June 1903, flashing a white signal every ten seconds. At the same time a red range light was added to warn of the dangerous Shagwong Reef.

Captain James G. Scott served as head keeper from 1885 to 1910. He was the first keeper at Montauk to wear an official keeper's uniform (Uniforms were instituted by the U.S. Lighthouse Board on May 1, 1884). He kept numerous accounts of weather, everyday life and lightkeeping activities, even shipwrecks that occurred at or near the lighthouse during his time at Montauk.

In 1907 an incandescent oil vapor lamp replaced the old static kerosene lamp, and in 1912 the keeper's dwelling was enlarged to create additional living space for the keeper's assistants. John E. Miller was the keeper at this time. He had been a police officer in Brooklyn for more than twenty years before coming to Montauk. During his term as lightkeeper (1912-1929) the Prohibition era began, and in 1925 Miller and his assistants were involved in an investigation alleging their involvement with the offloading of liquor from two vessels that came ashore in the vicinity of the lighthouse, the *Imperial* and the *Linnie Bell*. Though all were exonerated, the Lighthouse Service said it would "clearly observe this station and the keepers in the future for any evidence of collusion with the liquor traffic or intentional violation of the regulations of this service."[1]

Visitors became more numerous at the lighthouse in the late 1920s due to the development of Montauk by Carl Fisher beginning in 1926. The construction of the Montauk Point State Parkway in 1931 by Robert Moses to provide access to the new Montauk Point State Park greatly improved access to Montauk Lighthouse as well and brought more visitors.

In 1934 a concrete road was constructed from the main road up the hill to the keeper's dwelling and a central hot water heating system was installed. Electric power lines reached the keeper's dwelling in 1938, providing lighting, heating, and indoor plumbing.

In 1939 the U.S. Bureau of Lighthouses was absorbed into the Coast Guard, ending the tradition of the civilian keeper and instating Coast Guard keepers. The last three civilian keepers at Montauk—Thomas Buckridge, Jack Miller, and George Warrington—were gone by 1943. The lighthouse itself was modernized by the Coast Guard in 1940 when a 1000-watt halogen bulb replaced the incandescent oil vapor lamp. A radio beacon also was installed at this time. Thereafter, all keepers were Coast Guardsmen.

The three keepers who served at the Montauk Point Lighthouse from 1930-1943. Head keeper Thomas Buckridge, left; 1st assistant Jack Miller, center; 2nd assistant George Warrington, right. (Montauk Point Lighthouse Museum)

Chapter 1

The Keepers and Their Families

....spent many an hour on Turtle Hill by the old lighthouse, on the extreme point, looking out over the ceaseless roar of the Atlantic.

Walt Whitman
"Paumanok, and My Life on it as Child and Young Man"
Specimen Days

Thomas Abel Buckridge (1874-1955)

The history of the Buckridge family and their association with lighthouses begins with John Nind Buckridge who was born in New York City on June 12, 1833. He married Margaret Ann Abel (born October 15, 1837) in New York City on December 24, 1860.

According to Buckridge's granddaughter, Margaret Buckridge ("Bucky") Bock, John was in the Navy in his late teens. He sailed aboard the *North Carolina* in early 1852, later transferring to the Brooklyn Navy Yard to the store ship *Supply*, commanded by Lieutenant Commander Arthur St. Clair, attendant to Commodore Perry's expedition to the China Sea and Japan. The supply ship was the first to leave China for Japan, where the Treaty of Friendliness was signed on March 31, 1854. Buckridge, along with two other seamen, were the first Americans to spend time in Japan after the signing of the treaty.

John Nind Buckridge was discharged as an ordinary seaman on February 17, 1855 and enlisted for the Paraguay Expedition up the LaPlatte River, sailing from Norfolk, Virginia on January 2, 1856 aboard the U.S. Frigate *St. Lawrence*. He was discharged as an able seaman on May 21, 1859.

By 1860 he was working as a clerk in the West Farms section of the Bronx, New York. With the outbreak of the Civil War, he joined the 135th Regiment, New York Volunteers, 6th New York Heavy Artillery on August 19, 1862, commanded by Captain Kibbe. On March 28, 1864 he was seriously injured while on a woodcutting detail at Brandy Station near Rappahannock, Virginia. He was transported to the Armory Square Hospital in Washington, D.C. where his right leg was amputated. He was discharged on July 20, 1865.

John ran a food market on Main Street in West Farms, New York for a few years before purchasing it outright from John Butler on July 12, 1869. He sold it to John Adams Jr. on March 11, 1877 for $350.

It was at this point that 43-year-old John Nind Buckridge began his career in the lighthouse service. A wooden leg created challenges for a lightkeeper, but it was no deterrent to getting the job. The Lighthouse Service regularly employed disabled veterans as compensation for their war injuries. John was assigned to the Stepping Stones Lighthouse as an assistant keeper on October 1, 1877 at an annual salary of $450.00. The lighthouse site—a haphazard scattering of stones between the mainland and Long Island—supposedly was named by the Siwanoy Indians who claimed the stones were tossed into Long Island Sound by a devil trying to make his escape from the angry tribe. For many years, maps referred to the area as the "Devil's Belt."

At Stepping Stones Lighthouse Buckridge met Captain James G. Scott who was second assistant keeper and would later become head keeper at the Montauk Point Lighthouse. Buckridge was transferred to the Stratford Shoal Lighthouse, in Long Island Sound near Bridgeport, Connecticut, on September 26, 1878 also as an assistant keeper. On March 1, 1881 he moved to the Eaton's Neck Lighthouse, enclosing Long Island's Northport Bay, again as an assistant keeper.

On June 26, 1883 he became the head keeper of the Lynde Point Lighthouse marking the mouth of the Connecticut River at Old Saybrook, serving until he retired in 1902. Although his son Thomas assisted in operating the light for his aging father, according to Bucky Bock, her grandfather "was not as handicapped as one would think, because my father recalls being caught when my grandfather chased him." At pleasant Lynde Point she said her grandfather "was able to have his family with him. My father [Thomas], who was nine years old at that time and who lived with his parents in the lighthouse until he married, was initiated into lighthouse keeping at an early age. He did most of the climbing for his father, who must have found it difficult to climb those tower stairs with a wooden leg."[2]

In 1886 John Buckridge purchased a home on Seaside Avenue in Westbrook, Connecticut, where he spent his retirement years. The wooden leg finally began to give out and John was eventually confined to an "invalid chair." He died in Westbrook on January 23, 1912 at age 78 and was buried in the town's Cypress Cemetery. His wife Margaret died on February 15, 1920 in New Haven and was buried beside her husband.

John and Margaret had six children:
Elizabeth Ann (1861-1869). She died after falling from her horse.
Minnie (1868-1937)
Eliza Jane, nicknamed Lida (1871-1951)
Martha Washington (1876-1959)
Thomas Abel (1874-1955)

A second Elizabeth Ann was born May 6, 1879, but died four days later. Thomas Abel, born January 21, 1874 at West Farms, eventually followed in his father's footsteps and joined the lighthouse service.

Thomas's education was considerable for the times. He completed a year of high school and a year at Connecticut Business College. In 1893 he was employed at the Dickinson Witch Hazel Company in Essex, Connecticut. In 1900 he was living with his parents at the Lynde Point Lighthouse where he assisted his father.

John Nind Buckridge, right, at Lynde Point Lighthouse, ca. 1895. Son Thomas, center, assisted his father for many years here, eventually joining the lighthouse service himself. (Margaret Buckridge Bock)

Thomas married Sarah ("Sadie") Jeannette Tucker (born April 23, 1876 at Essex) in her mother's house on Collins Lane in Essex on March 28, 1901. After about a year they built a home next to her mother. By 1904 Thomas was working for Comstock and Cheney Company. He also worked as a boat builder for Frank Harrison for seven years. Given the nickname "Captain," he worked in a factory in the winter in Essex and for twelve summers he was a commercial fisherman at Montauk with his boat, *Jacky*. While at Montauk, his family lived in a primitive dwelling at Fort Pond Bay, constructed of fish packing crates.

Thomas took the lighthouse keepers examination on February 7, 1922. Among his skills included on the application were carpentry and painting. On May 4th he entered the lighthouse service assigned as keeper at Execution Rocks Lighthouse, off Sands Point in western Long Island Sound, to replace James F. Mulvey who resigned the position. Thomas' salary was $780, which was raised to $840 on July 1st.

On December 11, 1922 Thomas Abel Buckridge wrote to the Superintendent of Lighthouses about a transfer to Race Rock Lighthouse in Long Island Sound off Fishers Island:

> *If the vacancy expected comes around the first of January I will accept it. The reason for this is that this keeper here and I get along together very nicely and he has a new 2nd and my transfer earlier than that would mean leaving him with two new men, and as I know the amount of work connected with this station, I would rather lose the*

opportunity if the vacancy cannot wait until time stated, than leave him with two inexperienced men.[3]

Head keeper at Montauk Point Lighthouse, Thomas A. Buckridge, date unknown. Buckridge performed his duties well over a 22-year career in the Lighthouse Service. (Margaret Buckridge Bock)

His request apparently was granted, as Buckridge was transferred to Race Rock Light on January 1, 1923, replacing keeper Joseph Maynard who resigned. Buckridge's salary was set at $900, in part due to the remoteness of the lighthouse, a caisson-style, sea-swept sentinel built on a submerged rock ledge in "The Race," a swift current created by the bottleneck between the mainland and Fishers Island. Less than a year later Buckridge's pay rate was raised to $1080 and eventually to $1980 on July 1, 1928.

Bucky Bock recalled the rugged life her father lead at Race Rock:

[It] was a treacherous spot; sometimes it was so rough that it would be a week before he or the assistants could get to the island for their mail and fresh food. The dwelling of this lighthouse was similar to a house on land except that the furnishings were sparse. The short tower was approached from the second floor bedrooms. The men were allowed 30 days leave a year, which boils down to about two and a half days a month that Dad was able to visit his family in Essex."[4]

On January 1, 1930 Thomas Buckridge transferred to the Montauk Point Lighthouse, replacing keeper John E. Miller who was retiring. He accepted a salary of $1680. It was a drop of $300 from his previous salary at Race Rock Light Station, but Montauk was much less dangerous and remote than Race Rock and also more habitable. Montauk was a station designed for families, and Thomas's wife was able to live with him. During his time at Race Rock, which was considered too isolated for women and children, she had remained home in Essex, seeing her husband only a few times a month.

Thomas and Sarah had four children:
 John Orson, nicknamed "Jack" (1901-1973)
Thomas Irwin, called "Irwin" or "Buck" (1907-1992)
Elizabeth (1913-2004)
Margaret Mary, nicknamed "Bucky", born September 24, 1919

Elizabeth was born June 22, 1913 at Essex. While at Montauk and before her marriage, she worked as a secretary for the Montauk Beach Development Corporation in the Montauk "skyscraper." She married Albert Crawford Santi (1912-1995) on May 15, 1938, the ceremony held in the keeper's dwelling at the Montauk Point Lighthouse. It was one of several weddings that would take place in the lighthouse over the coming years for couples seeking a beautiful and unique setting.

Elizabeth Buckridge Santi, daughter of keeper Thomas Buckridge (Margaret Buckridge Bock)

**Jonathan Allen Miller, keeper of Montauk Point Lighthouse
1865-1869, 1872-1875 (Montauk Point Lighthouse Museum)**

John Allen "Jack" Miller (1891-1969)

When Thomas Buckridge arrived at Montauk Light in 1930, Jack Miller had been working as the first assistant keeper since November 1, 1917 under head keeper John E. Miller, his father.

The Miller family was long established on Long Island's east end, dating from the family's move from Massachusetts to Southampton about 1643 and the arrival of John Miller in East Hampton in 1649, only a year after its settlement. He was among the first settlers. (See the Appendix for a list of his descendants.) Jack's grandfather,

Jonathan Allen Miller, born in Springs, near East Hampton in 1834, married Margaret Burke on March 27, 1856 and they had fourteen children. He served in the Union navy during the Civil War, losing an arm in battle while aboard the ship *Onida*. He was the first Miller to be stationed at the Montauk Point Lighthouse, beginning as an assistant keeper on October 13, 1864, becoming head keeper on January 1, 1865, and serving until his transfer on May 13, 1869. He returned as head keeper on December 5, 1872 and served until October 15, 1875. He died October 29, 1915.

Jonathan Allen Miller's son, John Ellsworth, also served as a keeper at the Montauk Point Lighthouse. John was born May 2, 1863 and worked as a police officer in Brooklyn, New York for 23 years before becoming head keeper at Montauk on May 16, 1912. He worked in this capacity until December 31, 1929. He died February 28, 1932.

John Ellsworth Miller married Mary Alice Ledwith on October 4, 1887. They had six children, four of whom died in infancy and one at age two. The remaining child, John Allen ("Jack"), survived to adulthood and became the third Miller to be stationed at the Montauk Point Lighthouse.

John Ellsworth Miller, keeper at Montauk Point Lighthouse 1912-1929. He became keeper after serving over 20 years in the New York City police department. (Montauk Point Lighthouse Museum)

As early as May 10, 1911, twenty-year-old John Allen "Jack" Miller was listed as an assistant keeper in the Lighthouse Service, earning an annual salary of $480. He arrived at Montauk on November 1, 1917 as first assistant keeper with an annual salary of $564, which was raised a hefty 27% to $720 on November 1, 1918. The increase was due to the efforts of George Putnam, Superintendent of the U.S. Bureau of Lighthouses. Putnam fought not only for better pay and working conditions for lighthouse service employees, but also a pension plan. Miller's pay was raised several more times while he was stationed at Montauk Point, eventually reaching $1800 (less $240 for rent) on January 16, 1941.

From July 1, 1917 to June 30, 1919 the U.S. Bureau of Lighthouses was temporarily transferred to the Navy Department because of World War I. This did not affect Miller's status at Montauk, but a few lightkeepers around the nation either lost their assignments or were transferred to the armed services.

Jack Miller was born in New York City on February 19, 1891 and married Maude Irene Finch on November 20, 1911. They had three sons:

Eugene Ellsworth (1912-1982)
Richard Daniel (1928-1950)
Jonathan Allen, born May 29, 1924 and currently residing in Florida.

A fisherman by trade but with a desire to follow in the footsteps of his ancestors (he also had an uncle, Charles G. Miller who served at a life saving station on Long Island), Jack began his quest to join the lighthouse service by taking the civil service exam on April 18, 1911. Less than a month later, on May 10th, he was appointed assistant keeper at the Long Beach Bar Light Station near Greenport, Long Island at a starting salary of $480. The lighthouse marked the entrance to Peconic Bay. Miller's duties included "assisting keeping light, caring for station, cleaning, painting, etc."[5] It's quite possible he also spent considerable time rowing and chipping ice, since Long Beach Bar Light was a screwpile structure that could be accessed only by boat and was prone to heavy ice buildup in winter. During Miller's time at Long Beach Bar, an efficiency report noted that he "takes great interest" in his work, and based on his service his salary was considered "right, fair equivalent".[6]

During Miller's time at Long Beach Bar, the station experienced a near disaster on August 3, 1911 when the steamer *Shinnecock* grounded in a heavy fog. The captain of the *Shinnecock* had set a course for the Plum Island Lighthouse, which marked the North Fork of Long Island. Upon hearing the Plum Island fog signal, he set his course for the Long Beach Bar Light at the entrance to the bay, listening for its fog signal. But as the ship neared the lighthouse no fogbell was heard, so the skipper continued his cautious forward progress. Moments later the *Shinnecock* ran aground directly in front of the lighthouse! The keeper finally activated the signal thirty minutes later and continued operating after the fog had lifted. Though the ship and passengers came through unscathed, the keeper in charge, William Chapel, was severely reprimanded.

After serving about a year and a half at Long Beach Bar Light, Jack Miller resigned from the Lighthouse Service effective December 7, 1912, for reasons unknown. However, circumstances changed for Miller in the ensuing months and he found himself back in the lighthouse service. On July 5, 1913 he rejoined as assistant keeper at the Rockland Lake Light Station in the Hudson River, again at $480 salary. He must have found life at this lighthouse a bit "off." The cast-iron, conical light tower, situated in the middle of the river, leaned about 9 inches out of plumb, its foundation having shifted a few years after it was constructed in 1894.

Rockland Lake Lighthouse had an unstable foundation and began to lean soon after it was commissioned in the Hudson River in 1894. Jack Miller served as assistant keeper at this light for three months in 1913. (Coast Guard Archives)

Again, Miller requested a change of scenery. After serving at Rockland Lake only two months, he wrote to his superiors: "I had a letter from James H. Bentley 1st assistant at Plum Beach Light, dated August 8th 1913, stating that he would like to exchange stations with me, and as we are both willing to exchange, we ask your kind permission to be transferred".[7]

The Lighthouse Service complied, and on October 16, 1913 Jack Miller began service as assistant keeper at the Plum Beach station, established in 1899 to aid navigators safely through the West Passage of Narragansett Bay in Rhode Island. He served here for over two years until he was transferred and promoted to the position of keeper at the Whale Rock Lighthouse,* located a few miles south of Plum Beach Light at the entrance to the West Passage of Narragansett Bay. His salary at Whale Rock was $648 per year.

However, just seven months later, and at his request, he was transferred to the Bridgeport Harbor Light Station in Connecticut on August 19, 1916. It was similar in design to the Long Beach Bar Light Station. At this assignment, Miller also was responsible for operation of the Bridgeport East Breakwater Light. In spite of the added responsibilities, his salary inexplicably dropped to $564.

Jack Miller continued on the move. On July 1, 1917 he became an assistant keeper at the Point Judith Lighthouse in Rhode Island, replacing William E. Gilmore who resigned his position. Miller's salary was now $540—less than his previous post—but his feet were firmly planted on the mainland and his family could reside with him. (Most of Miller's earlier assignments had been "stag stations," barring women and children.) Perhaps Point Judith was not to his liking, for he served here only four months. On November 1, 1917 Miller was transferred to the Montauk Point Light Station as first assistant keeper, replacing Harry G. Broadbrook who had resigned. Miller's salary was set at $564 per year.

Ditch Plains Coast Guard Station. Montauk keeper Jack Miller's cousin Milton Miller was stationed here when the Coast Guard took over operation of the Montauk Point Lighthouse. Photo taken August 16, 1941. (Margaret Buckridge Bock)

After serving at six light stations over a period of about six years, Jack Miller found his niche. He served as first assistant at Montauk Point for over twenty-five years until he retired. According to Bucky Bock, when her father Thomas became head keeper at Montauk in 1930, Miller was "disappointed that he wasn't made head keeper and I don't know why he wasn't. He resented this. They got along to an extent, but he did everything possible to annoy my father, like taking off without signing out. He was often antagonistic toward my father and did not make life easy for him."

George Washington Warrington (1901-1955)

George Washington Warrington was born in Selbyville, Delaware on November 6, 1901, the son of George and Addie Lynch Warrington. He enlisted in the Navy on June 24, 1920 and served as seaman 2nd class aboard the USS *Nevada* and USS *Wyoming*. He was discharged from the service on August 25, 1921. He married Esther Hoffeister around 1924 and they had two children, Louise and George Washington, Jr.

On August 25, 1925 he enlisted in the Coast Guard and served as a surfman at two life saving stations on Long Island's south shore—Point O'Woods (opposite Patchogue) and the Blue Point Station, both on Fire Island. He was discharged on August 24, 1927.

He endeavored to join the Lighthouse Service and on November 16, 1928 was advised that he was under consideration for a position at the Montauk Point Lighthouse station. He was told he would have to provide his own furniture, "except kitchen range."[8] His appointment was made official in a letter from the Service on December 24th, stating he "had been selected for the position of 2nd Assistant Keeper...and in accordance therewith are hereby directed to report for duty... Show this letter to the Keeper...which will be his authority for assigning you to duty. The name and address of the Keeper is John E. Miller, Montauk, Long Island, N.Y."[9] Warrington's salary was set at $1260 per year.

Warrington wasted no time reporting, as indicated in a letter to the Superintendent: "I taken [sic] the first North bound Express and have reported hear [sic] at Montauk Pt. Sta. for duty this afternoon, Dec. 26, 1928."[10] He replaced James Kirkwood, who was transferred, and moved into the main floor apartment on the north side of the Montauk Light keeper's dwelling.

Although Warrington's appointment was probationary, due to expire in June 1929, he performed his duties well, for on May 1, 1929 keeper Miller wrote to the Superintendent that Warrington's service "has been satisfactory and I consider him a suitable man to receive a permanent appointment."[11]

Warrington's annual salary was raised to $1,560 (less $240 for rent) on January 1, 1931.

George Washington Warrington in formal attire at Montauk Point Lighthouse, August 27, 1936. (Margaret Buckridge Bock)

Chapter 2

Life at the Lighthouse

The public's perception of the lighthouse keeper is that of a competent, kindly man. He is largely seen as a favorite uncle, puttering around a lighthouse, telling sea stories, and worrying about the dark.

Dennis L. Noble
Lighthouses and Keepers

When Thomas Buckridge began his career as head keeper at Montauk Point Lighthouse on January 1, 1930 it was an ambivalent time for his family. They looked forward to being reunited but worried about leaving behind good friends. Unlike the lighthouses at Execution Rocks and Race Rock, Montauk had a dwelling and the keeper's family could reside with him. When Buckridge first informed his family of the transfer, daughter Bucky recalled, "[I] didn't know whether to jump for joy or to cry, so I did both. I couldn't bear to leave my friends, and yet the idea of living in a lighthouse was overwhelming. One of my friends gave me a surprise party before I left on March 15, 1930… My sister did not come to Montauk until June because she wanted to finish out her school year."[12]

"Now that a car was a necessity rather than a luxury," Bucky said, "Dad bought a Model T (an antique even then), learned to drive, and moved mother and me to Montauk in March of 1930… As my two brothers were married by this time, they came to Montauk with their families to visit only. Our first trip from Essex to Montauk took 12 hours; we were later able to make it in 5 ½ to 6 hours as cars and highways improved."[13]

For those first two months before Buckridge brought his family to the lighthouse, Bucky "wondered how he managed since he didn't have any furniture yet. He may have gotten a couch from somewhere to sleep on. You don't think of those things."

After her graduation from high school, Bucky's sister Elizabeth went to work for the Montauk Beach Development Company in the office building in town. At that time, Bucky claimed, only the first two floors of the building were finished, plus the penthouse which had been used by developer Carl Fisher. The sisters used to play tennis at the huge tennis building located below the Montauk Manor, which had clay courts.

The Lighthouse Site

Bucky Bock described the living quarters at Montauk in detail:

We had four stories of living space on the keeper's side of the house. The basement was our kitchen-dining room. It was furnished with a large dining room table, a kitchen table, many chairs, a couch, my father's desk (his office), a coal-burning stove, a black iron sink with a hand pump and a kitchen cabinet with a built in flour sifter. This was the only counter space. There was a dark and dismal pantry [today's kitchen for the lighthouse museum staff] and an even darker storage room. Later, we had a bottled gas stove (mostly for summer use) and a gas refrigerator, which never worked too well because of the low ceiling. All illumination was by kerosene lamp. To go outside to the privy, one had to climb several steps to the kitchen door and pick up the key hanging nearby. In the summer time the screen door was always loaded with flies waiting to get inside.[14]

We had a little apartment building of privies also, one for each family- side by side- and always locked, as they were not for the general public.[15]

The first floor had the living room in the front of the house and my parent's bedroom in the back. In the living room we had several pieces of wicker furniture, a rocking chair, a piano, a small center table with an oil lamp and a small radio. We could only get WTIC, but as long as we could get Lowell Thomas and Amos & Andy, that was all that mattered.

The second floor had two large bedrooms, each with a double bed and a cot size bed, a dresser and a washstand. My room was decorated in pink and green (I can't stand pink to this day), and my sister's room was blue. The third room was only large enough for a twin size bed and a dresser and eventually became our bathroom.

The attic was a great storage place, but it also was handy for rainy-day play and occasional extra sleeping space when the house was overcrowded with company.[16]

Winters could be harsh. According to Bucky, the family maintained a pot-bellied stove in the living room. "The second floor was unheated. In the winter my sister and I took hot-water bottles to bed with us, and in the morning we usually dressed by the pot-bellied stove in the living room. Sometimes there was a fringe of ice in the water pitchers in the morning."[17] It also was noted that the fireplaces in the house were boarded up.

According to East Hampton historian Jeannette Edwards Rattray, the décor of the rooms in the dwelling "presents no problem, for the United States prescribes battleship gray for the walls and flat white for the woodwork, a color scheme to which even the women become inured finally. There are no locks on the doors, merely latches."[18]

Keeper Jack Miller's son, Jonathan, said in an interview:

The head keeper had the whole one side of the house, a two-story apartment so to speak, and had a basement kitchen. Every year we used to have a machinist come out from the Staten Island lighthouse service to overhaul the engines. He would stay a week or so and they had to board him while he was there. That's why they [the Buckridge family] had the extra space. We had the upstairs apartment on the other side of the house and the Warringtons had the lower one.

Regarding the everyday life, Bucky Bock said:

I enjoyed the storms and would spend hours watching the surf break against the rocks. In the spring the migrating birds, attracted by the light, would crash against the tower to their death. One year I buried over a hundred of these dead birds. In the spring we would pick arbutus somewhere near the fishing village- now on the restricted list. We also used to pick wild cranberries in the meadows near the lighthouse, and blueberries, too, although I don't remember just where they grew. Mother always made jam from the fruit of a beach plum bush that grew just outside the living room entrance. We always had to check for ticks after these excursions, said to have come to Montauk with the sheep in the early days of the three houses.[19]

Jonathan Miller echoed Bucky's pastime memories: "We were busy in school and doing homework most of the time, but on weekends, especially in summer months when the season was right, we'd go out blueberrying and blackberrying. And in September, cranberrying."

Bucky described everyday activities:

We had a small garden in the hollow outside the kitchen door. Nothing grew too well in that sand, but mother did have a few flowers and vegetables from it. Laundry was a major event every Monday. All the water had to be heated on the stove, of course. Dad would set up the wringer with a washtub on each side, and using the old washboard, Mother would scrub away. Sometimes, if Dad's chores didn't take him away, he would help her. Lines were put up near the garden and were taken down afterwards because of the visitors.

Garbage collection? Unheard of. The papers were burned, and the garbage was thrown over the bank. In fifteen minutes it was all gone- disposed of by the scavenger gulls.

We did most of our shopping in East Hampton. One time, we got home and discovered a bag of meat that didn't belong to us. My father went right back to the store on Newtown Lane (the A & P?) and returned it."[20]

Bucky joked about her father's actions in 2007: "I wouldn't do it! I would have put it in the freezer!" But she did acknowledge that her father was a very honest man.

Bedroom of Thomas and Sarah Buckridge. A cozy room, the glass display case by the window was once a closet and a sewing machine sat beneath the window. Today the room contains exhibits about the erosion problem at Montauk Point, dedicated to the memory of Giorgina Reid. February 2008. (Author Photo)

The parlor of the head keeper's quarters. During Thomas Buckridge's time at Montauk, this room featured an upright piano and a potbellied stove in front of the fireplace. The glass display case at left was once a closet. February 2008. (Author Photo)

The passageway. This "breezeway" connected the keeper's dwelling with the oil room (left) and the radio room (right). November 2007. (Author Photo)

Trips were made to East Hampton every Saturday for food shopping. Bucky Bock remembered other travels for the family:

We could buy clothing in East Hampton also, but sometimes we went to Sag Harbor or traveled 50 miles to Riverhead for a better selection and a better price tag. Even more frequently, clothing was ordered from Sears-Roebuck's or Montgomery-Ward's catalogs.

Someone tried to get to the post office every day. It used to be in the fishing village near Jake's Fishing Market. Later, I believe, it was in the 'shopping center' near White's Drug Store. We did have milk delivered to us three times a week. We got the East Hampton Star by mail, but most of our other news was from the radios, unless someone happened to pick up a paper when they were in the village."[21]

At that time Bucky said Montauk village contained "a drug store, a food store, a few restaurants, and a few gas stations.[22]

Jonathan Miller spoke of his father's favorite pastimes while at Montauk: "My father was a great fisherman. He used to have a fishing stand out in front of the bluffs out there. He would go down there and surf cast. He liked the exercise. He used to make his own jigs (fish lures). In winter months he would fix up his rods and reels. He always had something to keep himself busy."

A part of life at the Montauk Point Lighthouse was the presence of fog, sometimes very dense fog, as noted by Bucky Bock:

I hear people talking about foggy weather. Nobody has any conception of fog unless they have lived at the Montauk Lighthouse. Sometimes, the fog engines would run steadily for a week or ten days. All the pictures on the walls would be crooked. When the horns finally stopped, it would feel as though the whole world had come to an end. If we were caught away from the station during a heavy fog, the driver of the car often would have to keep his head out of the window to get any visibility at all. Of course, we always had 'fog lights' on the car. It was during three different occasions like this that my sister hit deer with her car, usually when she was coming home from work just before she entered the wooded area coming down the second big hill.[23]

Concerning the fog signal she said, "The sound of it was something we got used to. We just didn't hear it after a while."

On January 20, 1936 the fog signal was changed to a diaphragm air horn with a different tone than the former signal. The two horns emitted a blast every fifteen seconds, lasting two seconds.

Montauk Point Lighthouse. Note railing in foreground, visitors, and foghorn. Photo taken August 10, 1937. (Margaret Buckridge Bock)

36

For many years the Montauk Point Lighthouse was a lonely and isolated place to live. For decades, the nearest town of any size was the village of East Hampton, twenty miles away. It wasn't until the 1920s, when a paved road was built across the long dreary "Napeague Stretch," that Montauk was open to the world.

When asked about the isolation at the lighthouse in 1933, Thomas Buckridge's wife, Sarah, said: "It isn't so lonely. We have many friends at the village and there are church and other affairs. Then, the people who come here to see the light make things interesting."[24]

For many years Montauk Point was indeed a lonely and desolate location. Even the drive to the lighthouse could be an eerie, yet beautiful experience as seen in this view of the Old Montauk Highway not far from the Point in 1924. (Photo by Eugene Armbruster. The Queens Borough Public Library, Long Island Division, Eugene L. Armbruster Collection)

School Days

Upon her arrival at Montauk, Bucky Bock discovered that the schools in New York were quite different than those in Connecticut. She recalled:

The work of the fifth and sixth grades was completely interchanged. I hadn't the slightest idea of the new work, nor how to find time to do it...I managed, however, by hard work to bring my average up to a tie for the highest place in June.[25]

My fifth grade teacher was Mrs. Hickling. Although always a good scholar, I found changing schools in March tough going. The curriculum was very difficult... Moreover, I just couldn't seem to get all the assignments done in school the way we had in Connecticut. Finally, I asked if I could take some books home (a no-no in Connecticut). Mrs. Hickling was flabbergasted to learn that I had been trying to do all the work in school, as the intent had been 'homework'. For my sixth, seventh and eighth grades I had Carleton Farrell as teacher and principal. School was a cinch in the sixth grade, having really done both the fifth and sixth grade curriculum in the fifth grade.

I spent a good part of the time working on an ancient typewriter in the library, typing the school newspaper [the Sea Breeze]. Ralph Pitts used to tease me by saying it was at least five minutes between bells on the typewriter to signify the end of a line. There were about twelve in my fifth grade class, but by the time I graduated from eighth grade, only Milton Bevis, Knowles Smith and I were left. We still had a full graduation ceremony with each of us giving separate speeches. Years later, visiting the school, I was told by Mr. Farrell that he was still using my geography notebook to correct his current students' workbooks. Most of the students were well-behaved, but I recall a few being punished with the 'rubber hose'.

Recess consisted of playing softball, using the swings and seesaws, playing 'jack-knife' or free play. My best friends were Louise Hoerger, Lavinia Warner, Anna Hedges and Joyce Appleyard... A big treat was to run over the hill after lunch to Wallace's store and buy a few pennies' worth of candy. In the winter we played in the gym- either basketball or a game with rulers. Basketball was a new experience for me, as we did not have gyms in our Connecticut elementary schools at that time. By the sixth grade I was an established member of the team, which was coached by Peggy O'Neill from Amagansett and was undefeated during those years.

School was a drastic change for Bucky Bock in another way. In Connecticut she could walk to and from school and even come home for lunch, but at Montauk Point Lighthouse:

I took the bus from the foot of the hill [at the lighthouse] at 7:30am and returned home about 5:00pm. We used...[Old Montauk Highway] to pick up the Smith children, then went to Star Island to pick up the Aarseth children, then to the Ditch Plains Coast Guard Station for Lavenia Warner and a bunch of younger children. Next, we picked up the Sears children in the village and few children living on the road along Fort Pond. After leaving us at school, Mr. Hedges picked up another bus load of children at the fishing village.

Jonathan [Miller] went on the bus with us. [George] Warrington had George Warrington Jr. and Louise with us. In the early days before I knew anyone I would play with them in the yard with their trucks.

The sixth grade class of 1931-32 poses in front of the Montauk School. Margaret Bock is second from left in bottom row. (Margaret Buckridge Bock)

In September 1933 Bucky attended the high school in East Hampton, riding 22 miles on the bus:

Mr. Hedges dropped us off in Montauk village to wait for Mr. Parsons, the high school bus driver. Often, we went into the poolroom at the end of the 'shopping center' and had a game or two while we waited."[26] This poolroom had previously been a hardware store operated by Mr. Honey and he had later converted it into the poolroom.

We always raced for the bumpy rear seat to take fullest benefit of the 'thank-you-ma'ams' on the second portion of the old road [Old Montauk Highway], for we had the Miller children, the Dickinson children, and Alice Hawley to pick up on this road. Anyone who misbehaved was put off the bus to get home the best way possible. It was usually not difficult to get a ride as 'hitch hikers' posed no threat then.
In order to participate in any school activities, someone in my family had to come to East Hampton to get me. Since that was not always possible, I frequently stayed overnight with friends Mae Carde in East Hampton and Winifred Parsons and Doris Zenger in Amagansett. But most of the time I stayed at the Briggs' home on Coopers Lane, often with no notice for them. If no one picked me up, I went there and Mrs.

Briggs always found something for me to eat even if the rest of the family had finished their evening meal and, of course, a place to sleep.

I was a cheerleader and a member of the basketball team, again a four year champion team. I was also able to go to many parties and dances because of these friends. Incidentally, the big kitchen at the lighthouse was a great place to have a party when I wanted to reciprocate the many invitations I had had.[27]

Bucky Bock graduated from East Hampton High School on June 20, 1937 as salutatorian in a class of forty-five students. She finished with a 95.1 average, missing valedictorian by 0.5 to her friend Winifred Parsons.

Margaret Bock celebrating high school graduation at the lighthouse, June 1937. (Margaret Buckridge Bock)

Neighbors and Social Life

Given the isolation of Montauk and the small population of permanent residents in the 1930s, it is easy to understand how people came to know each other well. Traveling east of Montauk village there were a small number of homes at the time and lighthouse neighbors were few. Bucky Bock recalled:

Our nearest neighbors were a mile or so away. The Hedges lived on the sound line. The road to their house was near the Spanish adobe building, then the barracks and home of the resident State Trooper. Wilson Hedges was the school bus driver; his wife was Gladys and his daughter Anna.

Annie and Joe Clark, Gladys's parents, lived with them also. Anna was a year or so younger than I was. She taught me much of the skills of basketball and we used to practice by the hour in her 'gym' on the second floor of her father's barn. Mrs. Clark ran the concession stand in the state park located near the base of the highway circle.'[28]

Bucky said that the stand was situated in the middle of present Montauk Point State Park and mostly sold hot dogs and a few souvenirs. "It was just a little shack and then they built her the home, the restaurant, at the top of the hill where the state trooper is now." She recalled:

On the other side of the island and on the old road were the Smiths- Knowles Sr. and Jr.- Mary and her mother. They ran the Wyandanee Inn and the Ocean View Inn (near the Hither Hills Coast Guard Station), where I also worked as a waitress one summer. Knowles, the son, was a classmate of mine. They usually went to Florida in the winter. I never worked at the Wyandanee Inn. It was located on the Old Montauk Highway. The Smiths would have church functions there every now and then, card parties, something like that. Mary Smith [Fullerton] is a lovely person. She's one of the few people left that I would know [now living on Montauk].

When asked if her family ever went to the inn for dinner she replied:

We never ate out. The only time I ever ate out with my parents was when we took a trip after I graduated from high school and we ate at a few restaurants. We never had the money to eat out.[29]

One of the neighbors was Lathrop Brown (1883-1959), who was a New York State representative in Congress and also held several other government positions. His estate was located across from the Wyandanee Inn on the Old Montauk Highway, the centerpiece of which was a beautiful old windmill. Bucky spoke fondly of visits there:

The estate was a beautiful place and they were lovely people. We weren't very close with them but they did invite us a couple of times a year for tea. They would have given us something stronger except my parents didn't drink. Every time my father would go to sit in a chair, Mr. Brown would say, 'Not there, Tom. That's a fragile antique.' My father was a big man. He always found a place to sit, however. The room we sat in was the first floor of the windmill. It was a beautiful room filled with antiques. Every year the Browns would have the handicapped veterans from World War I come out for a weekend a couple of times. They were very nice people.[30]

Wyandannee Inn, Montauk Point, Long Island

Situated a short distance west of the lighthouse on the Old Montauk Highway, the Wyandanee Inn served tourists comfortably for many years. (Courtesy of the Queens Borough Public Library, Long Island Division, Postcard Collection)

In 1942 the estate was broken up and the windmill was relocated to make way for the development of Camp Hero. Bucky was happy to learn that the windmill still stands today, having been moved for the final time to Wainscott in 1952.

At the lighthouse, Bucky recalled the family entertaining plenty of company. On one occasion they had a number of family members come for dinner, filling both tables in the basement kitchen. A visitor peeked in the window and was heard to say, "I know it's a restaurant, but how do we get in there?"[31]

Bucky recalled:

When Dad's cousins from New York City came, they would always buy a steak, which we would cook in a fireplace made from the rocks on the beach. Dad preferred to eat crackers and milk, rather than suffer the lumpy rock seats on the beach. We also had a lot of company from Connecticut. They would come over from New London on the ferry to Montauk, and it was always a big event to go to meet them.[32]

42

We did occasionally visit at the Eaton's Neck Lighthouse [near Northport, Long Island]. There was a kinship among local lighthouse keepers. We also went to Staten Island to visit the man who used to be keeper at Race Rock with my father. He had three lighthouses that he took care of there [at Staten Island]. Together they made a triangle. He lived at one but took care of all three.

Entertainment at the lighthouse consisted of 'Amos & Andy' and Lowell Thomas on the radio. I should add here, too, that the church and the school were very much part of our social life at Montauk. There were dances, minstrel shows, plays, food sales, suppers, card parties, women's group, youth groups and other activities to keep us busy. However, I never had the opportunity to be a girl scout, as there was no scouting or other organized activity in Montauk, and East Hampton was too far away. However, we did not lack for entertainment.[33]

Margaret Buckridge poses proudly with her father at the lighthouse in 1936. (Margaret Buckridge Bock)

With regard to the Miller and Warrington families at the lighthouse, Bucky said: "We weren't social. You know, here I was, in high school, baby sitter age, and I was never asked to be a baby sitter. If they went any place, the kids went with them. They didn't partake in events in town. The [Montauk Community] church and the school were the centers of activity...something for all ages. We went to most of them but the Millers and the Warringtons didn't go. Their children did go to Sunday school with us at times."

Even when Bucky's sister Elizabeth was married in the lighthouse in May 1938 neither the Millers nor the Warringtons attended. "Just the family came," said Bucky.

Referring to her father, Bucky said, "My father was strictly against liquor! He and my mother were teetotalers. There was always a bottle—I guess it was rye—that he kept in a cabinet in the basement kitchen. Never opened! It was supposedly for snake bite. But no one ever got bitten by a snake so it was never opened." She laughed, adding: "It must have been well aged for whoever ended up with it!"

Bucky also recalled an incident at the Point with a family member:

After my sister got her driver's license, my father was no longer our sole means of transportation to the 'outside world'. She used to drive us to Lake Montauk to swim. But we still liked to swim in the surf at Turtle Cove, if it wasn't too rough. One time, my brother's sister-in-law, who was my age, was swimming there and got a fish hook caught in the fleshy part of her hand. Dad tried to remove it but it was hurting her too much. Luckily, that summer there was a doctor at the Montauk Manor; otherwise the nearest doctor was Dr. Edwards in East Hampton.[34]

Montauk in the 1930s

During 1930-31 the new Montauk Point State Parkway was constructed to the Point by WPA workers. It extended the full length of Montauk Peninsula, from Hither Hills to the lighthouse. Bucky joked that her father claimed the workers, "spent more time leaning on their shovels than digging, but it was a big improvement."[35] A favorite hike for Bucky was to walk as far as Third House on the new highway and then return via hilly Old Montauk Highway.

The 1930s was the era of the Great Depression. According to Bucky:

The government started charging us $15 a month rent, which was really a cut in salary. A few prices stand out in my mind: lamb was 15 cents a pound (we ate a lot of it); gas was 8 gallons for $1; swordfish at Jake's was 50 cents a pound. We had it as a treat, but mostly we ate the fish dad caught or got free from his fishermen friends at the docks. They gave him the fish that was bringing a low price or was not sellable, such as sea robins (which made a delicious fish chowder). We ate well, despite all, as my mother was a good cook. Of course, Saturday was baked beans night- the beans cooked all day in the coal stove.[36]

The 1930s also represented the last years of Prohibition in the United States. When asked how her father managed the station during a time when Montauk was heavily involved in the "rum running" trade, Bucky said, "My father wasn't exposed to the activities of Prohibition. But just between you and me, that's how a lot of local people got very wealthy!"

When asked about the problem with the eroding bluffs at Montauk Point, Bucky said: "They didn't talk about working on it, but when we were there a corrosion test was done on metals in an area that was out near the edge of the bluff. When we got there you could walk around it. But before we left it was falling over the bank. Quite a bit of… [the bluff] went down while we were there."

In 1933 alone, ten feet of land was lost. The *East Hampton Star* reported:

Mr. Buckridge has seen it break off the point, little by little, as lashing seas attacked the shore. Every year the point grows smaller and the ocean comes ever nearer to the lighthouse…But people are not yet thinking seriously of moving the lighthouse back.

There is a cement platform at the end of the flat plateau on the point. At one time an automobile company used this for display purposes, so it seems, for visitors were given a choice of fancy automobile door handles for their next year's model. Actually they were placed there for a scientific purpose, to test the durability of the finish under the changing activities of the elements. A few years ago this platform was placed well back from the edge of the cliffs; now one cannot walk around it, and soon it will topple into the sea.[37]

East Hampton historian Jeannette Edwards Rattray painted an ominous picture of the future of the Montauk Light Station in 1938, stating that the lighthouse was "less than 140 feet from the edge of the sheer cliff…the sea has eaten away the bank through the years. People who know something about such things claim that the light will last only about fifty years longer; then something will probably be put in the water to take its place."[38]

In the late 1960s, efforts by the Army Corps of Engineers, the Coast Guard and others had failed to halt the relentless onslaught of erosion at Montauk Point, and the future of the lighthouse was in doubt. Then, a sixty-one-year-old woman named Giorgina Reid spearheaded a campaign to save the lighthouse by terracing the bluff around the lighthouse property. In talking about Reid's efforts to halt the erosion, Bucky said: "She did a beautiful job and was an extraordinary woman. I never knew her. To think she was even interested in doing it! Really amazing!"

A view of the main street (Route 27) looking east in the hamlet of Montauk in 1929. Financial difficulties forced developer Carl Fisher to halt further construction at Montauk in late 1920s. Photo by Eugene Armbruster. (Queens Borough Public Library, Long Island Division, Eugene L. Armbruster Collection)

Montauk Point, the tip of that famous strip of land known as Long Island

Spectacular aerial view of Montauk Point in the early 1930s showing the windmill estate of Lathrop Brown in the distance and the Wyandanee Inn at upper right. Photo by Robert Y. Richie. (Montauk Library)

Chapter 3

Keeping a Good Light

"I think the keepers of lighthouses should be dismissed for small degrees of remissness, because of the calamities which even these produce."

Thomas Jefferson

"Keeping a good light" was the motto of a dedicated, hard-working lighthouse keeper. But to assure that light stations were properly maintained and due diligence was given to the operation of lighthouse equipment, periodic and unannounced Lighthouse Service inspections were conducted. Records of inspections during the 1930s at Montauk reveal that the station was basically kept in good order, but there were some problems. Assistant keeper George Warrington's son, George III, set an ominous tone about being prepared when he wrote in the 1930s: "Keep your fingers off the white paint—the Inspector is coming!"[39]

Duties of the Keepers

Paramount among lightkeeping duties was the overall appearance of the light station. It had to be clean, neat, and well-organized. Among the more tedious tasks was polishing the brass, of which it seemed most items were made. In the early 1930s at Montauk Lighthouse, electricity still had not come into use, so keeping up with cleaning away soot from kerosene fumes inside the lantern and on the Fresnel lens was a never-ending task.

According to Jonathan Miller, the three keepers on duty in the 1930s seemed to get along fairly well in matters of lighthouse maintenance: "The head keeper would come out early in the morning, about 8:00 or so, and they would meet in the engine room or some place like that where he would assign the work to be done that day; cut the grass, clean up, tend to the fog signal, painting to be done, something like that."

According to *New York Times* reporter Edward Adolphe, the Montauk keepers earned between $110 and $145 a month depending on grade. He wrote:

[T]hey take twelve-hour shifts in rotation, during which they are directly responsible for the working of the mechanism (the lights by night, the fog horns day and night when necessary). Besides this each man devotes six hours daily to cleaning, repairing and polishing, making an eighteen-hour day. Six hours of each twenty-four they may call their own, besides four full days off each month. Sometimes they drive to town on those days.[40]

In the 1930s, when many other mainland lighthouses had been modernized with electric lights, the lighthouse at Montauk Point was still without it. But electricity was not far away; as a matter of fact, it was only about five miles away. The village of Montauk, created by Carl Fisher in 1926, was equipped with the conveniences of heating, lighting and indoor plumbing. Yet, the light station seemed to operate without difficulty using the economical, yet volatile fuel, kerosene, introduced here in 1884.

A 1933 *East Hampton Star* article spoke favorably about the absence of electricity at the light: "At least one industry has not suffered in an age of technocracy. There is a reason for this, for electricity is fairly expensive and even Uncle Sam does not wish to be extravagant. It is that old standby, kerosene, that is used instead. Vaporized and mixed with air, it can produce a brilliant light indeed."[41]

According to Edward Adolphe,

Because there is no electric power at Montauk, a mechanical device is used to turn the light- a ninety-pound weight on a cable which unrolls and revolves the machine. The man on duty at night must rewind the cable, like an old grandfather's clock, every four hours. Should he be at the base of the tower and trouble develop, a thermostat system would sound a gong denoting that the temperature from the flame inside the light had gone too far above or below its operating limits. Then he would climb up and revolve the light by hand while another member of the crew, summoned by another gong, would undertake the repairs.[42]

Adolphe reported that dealing with the lack of electricity, plumbing or heating "do not sit well with the three lighthouse wives... Since kerosene lamps are used, the day literally ends at dusk. But even the women work so hard all day that early retirement is a pleasure. The children stay up somewhat later with their radios."[43]

According to Bucky Bock, before electrification of the light it usually took about a half hour to light the incandescent oil vapor lamp. She pointed out:

It had a mantle similar to that of a Coleman lantern and had to be handled gently to prevent it from breaking. Then, the weights had to be wound up to make the light revolve. The lens was carefully cleaned to make sure it was free of dust and fingerprints. The visitors were not allowed to touch the lens, but someone always managed to do so when the keeper was talking to someone else. During the day the light was covered with a linen cloth [to protect it from the sun]... There was also a red warning light at the level of the outside walkaround. When ships could see this, they knew that they were in danger of going ashore on Shagwong Reef"[44]

George Warrington preparing the oil vapor canister for operation, ca. 1938. (Montauk Point Lighthouse Museum)

Bucky noted the tediousness of keeping the Fresnel lens clean on a daily basis when she said of the polishing: "It seemed like they were up there forever doing that! They tried to keep the dust off and remove fingerprints, since some visitors would touch the lens... Sometimes the keeper would revolve the light a little bit so people could see what happens. Normally it didn't rotate during the day. The cloth was removed from the lens when visitors went up so they could see it."

By 1937 there were rumors that the beacon in the Montauk Point Lighthouse was to be automated and the property electrified. Such a change certainly would have made maintenance of the light easier for the keepers and diminished the threat of fire. But according to Superintendent J. T. Yates, the rumors were unfounded: "This office has never had any thought or intention of recommending that Montauk Point Light be changed to an automatic light. The importance of this light, together with the necessity of the maintenance of a powerful fog signal at this light station, would make such action impracticable."[45]

George Warrington lighting the lamp inside the Fresnel lens, ca. 1938. (Montauk Point Lighthouse Museum)

Regarding electrification, Yates stated: "The Long Island Lighting Company advised, informally, that they were contemplating extending their lines to Montauk Point, but no advice has been received from them as yet to the effect that their lines have been extended. If this line is completed, this office will recommend the installation of electric lights in the keeper's quarters, but...not for the operation of the fog signal, as electric operation of the fog signal will nearly double the cost over that of the oil engines which are now being used.[46]

At this time there also was talk of replacing the beacon in the lighthouse with a blinking light on a steel tower. The Department of Commerce claimed there was no such plan in the works. Congressman Robert L. Bacon said: "Montauk Point Light Station is an important feature in the system of aids to navigation of that section of our coasts... I do not find in our files any suggestion that its discontinuance or replacement with any other type of aid has even been suggested." However, Bacon also stated that since electric power lines were being extended to the Point, "it may be that electrification of the station…may be undertaken in due course as a desirable improvement."[47]

Probably the most precarious job for the keepers was maintaining the appearance of the light station with whitewash. As noted by Bucky Bock, the white parts of the tower were whitewashed every year and the distinctive brown band was painted every two to three years. To accomplish this, scaffolding was used. According to Bucky, it was a chore "no one really enjoyed. I remember once when [George] Warrington was at the bottom and [Jack] Miller and Dad were in the rig, some rope slipped or broke and they slipped sideways. Fortunately, no one was hurt, as they were able to right themselves somehow, but the whitewash had splattered all over everything."[48]

Jonathan Miller said of the whitewashing: "They used a type of cradle or gondola car which was attached to ropes on pulleys that was suspended from the deck at the top. They would lower the gondola all the way down and start from the bottom up. They would do the whitewashing, then do the red stripe around the middle with red lead paint. They did all that work themselves without hiring outside contractors. They had plenty of work to keep them busy around there!"

Needless to say, there was always something that required paint. In addition, keepers had to clean the fog signal engines and mow the huge lawn. "They had to mow the yard using the old fashioned push mower," said Bucky Bock. "It wasn't easy since this consisted of tough beach grass."

Jonathan Miller recalled an exciting part of lighthouse life that occurred each year:

There used to be a lighthouse tender that came around and they would anchor off Scott's Cove in line with Block Island northeast of the Point. There were less rocks in this area than others. They would come in at high tide, run a great big hose up the bank to where there were three great big tanks beside the engine house that they would fill with kerosene for the lantern. Every morning [the keeper] had to carry a 5-gallon jug of kerosene up to replenish what they used overnight.

The tender also brought extra supplies, parts for machinery, soap for cleaning. We used to call it 'GI soap' in the army. The last tender I remember seeing was in the late 1930s. It was quite a sight to see when it came.

In the event of damage or injury, a "Report of Damage to Property or Injury to Persons" form was filed. One such case occurred on December 24, 1936 when assistant keeper Jack Miller, while "wiping glycerin from the windows in lantern…slipped in some of it, which had run down on the iron deck." The nature of the injury was described as a "busted blood vessel and contusion of the left knee," which caused Miller to miss an unknown period of work time.[49]

An issue that caused friction between George Warrington and head keeper Thomas Buckridge occurred in December of 1933 when Warrington applied for extended time off ("leave") during the approaching Christmas holiday. He wished to take leave from December 19th to December 31st. In a letter to the Superintendent on December 1st, Buckridge advised that Warrington had "requested leave for the entire

Christmas vacation and as we all have children in school as well as he, I don't think he is entitled to it all, and it should be divided up equally."[50]

The letter appeared to open a can of worms for keeper Buckridge, for in a reply from Superintendent J. T. Yates on December 5th, Yates stated:

It is noted that the application of 2nd Asst Keeper Warrington for 13 days leave Dec. 19th to 31st is approved by you, but that in accompanying letter you state 'Do not think he is entitled to it all, and it should be divided up equally'. You are advised that the matter of amount of leave within the authorized allowance, and the particular time when leave may be taken by Assistant Keepers, is to be decided by Keepers according to status of work and other conditions at the station with which the keeper is necessarily familiar, it being expected that equal opportunity for leave will be afforded each assistant as well as the Keeper, and it is not intended that such matters be referred to this office..[51]

Buckridge apparently didn't realize he had the power to authorize time off for his subordinates. In a letter written on December 6th he wrote: "...it seems I am vested with the authority of granting leave or not if I think conditions warrant it. This is something I am very glad to know.[52]

Superintendent Yates, in a letter dated December 12th advised Buckridge to come to a satisfactory decision and not burden the Lighthouse Service with problems that should be resolved by head keepers:

Application for leave...submitted by Asst. Keeper Warrington, for the period Dec. 19th to Dec. 31st inclusive, 1933, is herewith returned to you with the request that you return it to this office promptly with your unqualified recommendation.[53]

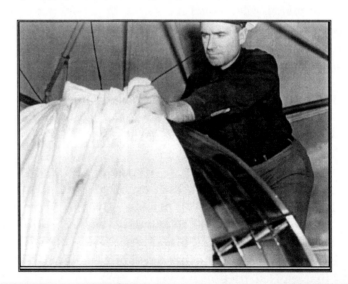

George Warrington performing his duties at Montauk Lighthouse, ca. 1938. Above, removing protective covering from Fresnel lens in tower. Next page, operating kerosene tank for incandescent vapor lamp. (Montauk Point Lighthouse Museum)

Finally, after seemingly endless correspondence between the Lighthouse Service and the keepers at Montauk, Warrington was refused leave until the evening of December 22nd, returning on the evening of December 31st. Keeper Buckridge made one last point to Superintendent Yates about Warrington on December 21st: "He knew I wanted to take four days around Xmas time to go see a new grand child, so he put this [request] in on the first of December to get his in first, to get it all".[54]

The remaining years at the Montauk Light Station appear to have been uneventful for Warrington as he no longer was the focus of letters to the superintendent.

Inspections and Recommendations

In the 1930s inspection forms rated lighthouse stations according to cleanliness, orderliness and operation, and keepers were evaluated by neatness, conduct, and efficiency. Both sets of ratings were based on a scale of one to one-hundred, with one-hundred being the best score. There was room for comments, including suggested repairs, replacements, improvements, procedures, equipment, and personnel.

The following are examples of inspections at Montauk. Thomas Buckridge always was listed as "keeper," Jack Miller as "1st Asst," and George Warrington as "2nd Asst."

On June 18, 1930 inspector O. C. Luther visited the lighthouse and recorded the following ratings:

Station: Cleanliness 90; Orderliness 90; Operation 95			
Personnel:	Neatness	Conduct	Efficiency
Buckridge	95	100	100
Miller		not seen	
Warrington	80	80	80

Remarks included a need for new floors (cost $250) in the keeper's kitchen, front hall and two rooms on the first floor (living room and bedroom), and heating plants ($1500) for the quarters of all three keepers. It was noted that, considering the short time he was in charge (6 months), Buckridge "has accomplished much improvement to station".[55]

On November 15, 1930, Luther again performed an inspection of the Montauk Light Station:

Station: Cleanliness 90; Orderliness 90; Operation 100			
Personnel:	Neatness	Conduct	Efficiency
Buckridge	90	90	95
Miller		not seen	
Warrington	90	90	90

Remarks included the need to clean the Shagwong Range light; also "wash from red, central band on tower has stained the white wash below." And "new floors are needed in kitchen, hallway and living room, keeper's quarters." Since Luther indicated that the keepers themselves would take care of the flooring, only the price of materials ($175) was noted.[56] The new flooring was installed in 1931.

Although first assistant keeper Miller was again "not seen," there was no indication of any inquiry as to his whereabouts.

Inspector F. W. Ockenfels conducted an inspection on June 12, 1931:

Station: Cleanliness 90; Orderliness 80; Operation 100

Personnel:	Neatness	Conduct	Efficiency
Buckridge	90	90	95
Miller	not present	80	75
Warrington	90	80	80

Remarks included:

Attic and basement in general disorder. All kinds of stuff said to belong to 1st Asst Miller in heaps and piles all thrown together. To be cleaned out and put in order.

Black paint spattered all over lantern glass, to be cleaned off. Floor in Asst's quarters shellacked which is worn and broken through. To be cleaned off and floors refinished. White paint on dwelling dirty and spotted.

Heating plants needed in quarters [cost $1500]. Sink water now drains out on ground. A small broken joint cesspool in the sand and gravel soil would readily carry off all water [$300]. General condition of station shows improvement under new keeper.[57]

In this inspection Ockenfels described the abilities of assistants Miller and Warrington, which gives us an idea of their work ethic:

1st Asst keeper Miller absent from station, but no record in Absence Book as required by Instructions. Keeper reports both assistants are slow workers. This station has 'drifted' for a long time, and they evidently did not relish the idea of the new keeper who set out to get work done that had been neglected. Warrington admitted that they previously had an easy time of it and that he had formed a mistaken idea of the new keeper when he came there, but had since changed his idea and was now getting along all right. He was told that both Assistants were expected to do their share to keep the station in proper condition, and if they didn't some one else would have to.

Embankment at Point is gradually wearing away due to sea and to a great extent to storm water running down the bank.[58]

Problems with Jack Miller's quality of work were noted prior to Buckridge's arrival at Montauk by the former head keeper, who lodged a complaint about him with the Lighthouse Service early in 1927. What is surprising is that the keeper at that time was John E. Miller, Jack's father! Superintendent J. T. Yates replied to the younger Miller:

> *You are advised that your explanation concerning your failure to make any attempt to accomplish or assist in accomplishing any of the painting work that had been ordered done on two different occasions is not by any means satisfactory. Your mere statement that there has been a number of odd jobs about the station that had to be attended to which prevented the accomplishment of the painting work ordered, indicates that your efficiency is far below that expected of first assistant keepers of Light Stations and also a lack of interest on your part in the position you hold as well as the work of the Service. You are hereby <u>cautioned</u> for your conduct as referred to herein and advised that you will be expected to show a very material improvement in your efficiency as first assistant keeper as well as interest in the work of the Station as otherwise further and more drastic disciplinary measures will be taken.[59]*

Problems continued for Miller with the arrival of Thomas Buckridge as head keeper in 1930, and by early 1931 charges of improper conduct were reported to the Lighthouse Service by Buckridge. The response from Superintendent Yates to Miller addressed several issues:

> *Your reply to charges of insubordination, disobedience of orders, and addressing contemptible and disrespectful language to a superior, is not by any means satisfactory. You admit that you refused to perform work as ordered by the Keeper, and state that you do not recall that you addressed the Keeper in language as stated in charges.*

> *In regard to your action in refusing to paint the ball on top of the lantern; you are advised that this or any other necessary work connected with the station that may be ordered done by the Keeper, is a part of the duties of the position you hold and for which you are paid, and so long as you occupy the position of Assistant Keeper you are expected to perform such duties, or if for any reason you are personally unable to perform items of work assigned to you that involve climbing, etc., you are expected to have such portions of your duties performed without expense to the Government, and this without refusal of duty, and without argument or dispute with the keeper, otherwise you are obviously unfitted for the position of Assistant Lighthouse Keeper....*

> *The fact that you have been cautioned will be made a part of your official history in the Lighthouse Service.[60]*

It appears that Miller's work improved, for a letter from the Superintendent six months later indicated "no further difficulties have been experienced due to insubordination, disobedience or other improper conduct".[61]

Luther inspected the Montauk Light Station on November 28, 1931 with the following results:

Station: Cleanliness 90; Orderliness 90, Operation 95

Personnel:	Neatness	Conduct	Efficiency
Buckridge	90	90	90
Miller		not seen	
Warrington	90	90	90

Among the remarks:

There is an old relic of an automobile which was left on station by former keeper [John E.] Miller [father of Jack Miller]. It was ordered removed from barn at last inspection and it was ordered off the reservation today.

The runway to barn is in poor repair and the barn floor is poor in spots. Keeper was ordered to repair both floor and run with lumber stored in barn cellar. The barn loft has a large store of jugs, corks, and other articles not needed for operating station and not needed by the keeper. Ordered them removed from the station.
[An interesting find, since these were the Prohibition years]

The keeper states that the assistants will now do what they are told and do it well but take their time about it. 2ⁿᵈ Asst states that things are going along well as far as he knows.

1ˢᵗ Asst Miller was absent on leave and could not be questioned. The keeper states that Miller could not work on the high jobs, he is good on the ground.[62]
[This may explain Miller's refusal to paint the ventilator ball atop the lantern earlier that year.]

Inspector Luther returned on May 27, 1932 and reported the following:

Station: Cleanliness 95, Orderliness 95, Operation 100

Personnel:	Neatness	Conduct	Efficiency
Buckridge	90	90	90
Miller	85	90	90
Warrington	95	90	90

The ratings were among the highest recorded during these years, as stated by Luther: "The station is in the best condition it has been during 22 years I have known it."

Nevertheless, there was a problem to correct: "The wooden shack on parapet deck which houses the Shagwong Reef light is getting poor and will need renewal in a year or two. Consideration should be given to shifting this lens to the lantern where there is ample room and the wooden shed can be eliminated".[63]

Despite the suggestion to relocate the range light, it took the Great Hurricane of September 21, 1938 to cause action. The storm severely damaged the light and its housing, necessitating its removal shortly thereafter to the safety of the interior of the lantern.

Though they managed to work together and maintain the overall operation of the light station, friction between Thomas Buckridge and Jack Miller flared up once again in the spring of 1932, this time because of allegations by Buckridge of false entries made by Miller in the Record of Absences. The matter was addressed in a letter from Superintendent J. T. Yates to Miller on June 6, 1932:

1...It is noted that while you verbally stated that you had not made false entries in the station records, your reply to charges...states that you "do not care to make any statement at the present" which in itself raises doubt in the matter and leads to the belief that, while not admitted, the charges may have some foundation of fact. Investigation of the matter, however, has not disclosed evidence to either prove or disapprove the charges, in view of which no further action will be taken at this time, but you are advised to exercise care...when making entries in Record of Absences or other station records...

2. Your countercharge...stating that the Keeper made false entries in Records of Absences on March 6, 1930...is entirely unsupported by any information or evidence to prove your charge. The fact that your charge is based on an alleged occurrence over two years ago and is unsupported by proof, indicates that your purpose was to bring discredit upon the Keeper...You are <u>hereby cautioned</u> for your action and disregard of service regulations in this instance and advised that a repetition will result in more drastic disciplinary measures being taken. The fact that you have been cautioned will be made a part of your official history.[64]

However, Superintendent Yates also admonished keeper Buckridge in a separate letter on the same day:

1. The subject of your letter of May 1, 1932 has been investigated, and it is found that you have no direct knowledge that the 1st Assistant Keeper has made false entries in the Record of Absences, and while it appears that the Second Assistant Keeper is of the belief that certain entries are not correct, there is no evidence to prove that such is the case. This condition necessarily places you in the position of having made charges which are unsupported by proof or evidence, and would indicate attempted oppression of a subordinate contrary to service regulations.

2. You are hereby <u>cautioned</u> for your action in making charges against the 1st Assistant Keeper without having adequate evidence or proof to support the charge, and advised that a repetition of this character will result in more drastic disciplinary measures being taken. The fact that you have been cautioned will form a part of your official history.[65]

Two visitors take a break at the terminus of the Old Montauk Highway opposite the Montauk Lighthouse in 1929. Photo by Eugene L. Armbruster. (Queens Borough Public Library, Long Island Division, Eugene L. Armbruster Collection)

The matter appeared to be put to rest in follow up letters by Assistant Superintendent F. W. Ockenfels in November 1932, which stated that no further problems had been experienced with either Buckridge or Miller and therefore no further actions were to be taken.[66] [67]

One can only imagine that for the duration of their time at the Montauk Light Station the relationship between Buckridge and Miller was difficult and at times stormy, and that their conversations were brief and only work-related.

Yet, troubles for the Montauk keepers continued. A revealing inspection of the light station by Superintendent Yates on July 26, 1933 nearly resulted in the removal of keeper Thomas Buckridge. In a stern letter to Buckridge on July 29, 1933 Yates presented the charges:

You are hereby charged with inefficiency and neglect of duty as Keeper of Montauk Point Light Station, New York, in that when the station was inspected on July 26, 1933 it was found that the engine room was dirty and cluttered; the engines were covered with grease, oil and dirt; the oil on the floor was so thick that many thicknesses of newspapers had been spread over the floor around the engines as well as waste and rags, and in one place where newspapers were saturated with oil boards were laid on the papers; drip pans and receptacles were full of oil, waste, oily newspapers and dirt, and a packing box full of oily newspapers, as well as several boxes of trash, old oil cans some with contents and some empty, paint cans, old tools, waste ends of material etc.

On the work bench in engine room there were several paint pots containing paint and in which brushes had been left and allowed to become stuck to the bottom of the pot. Amongst many sections of sectional ladders consisting of both good and bad sections, there were several pairs of paint covered overalls, which necessarily form a fire menace; the torches for heating engines were found to be improperly packed, they being so packed with wicking and so jammed with dirt that it was difficult to place the torches in operation;

the fog signal was permitted to remain inoperative for about four hours from 2:00 A.M. on July 21ˢᵗ, whereas it could have readily been kept in operation by pulling the valve lever by hand; the lens clock and lens pedestal were dirty, the clock especially being covered with oil and dirt; the lantern floor was dirty and not properly painted; a small bench used for holding small parts of lamp was dirty and cluttered, and underneath bench was found a bundle of old dirty rags, waste, and machine wipers; lantern window sash rusty; many window panes in lantern require renewal and no action taken to replace them although you were instructed to do so when station was last inspected;

practically no attention has been paid to the appearance of grounds, pathways having been cut by rain and wash waters and no action taken toward restoring paths or preventing further damage; no attempt has been made to maintain the small fence surrounding paint test panels which fence has fallen down and lies in a broken and tangled condition.

The only portion of the station that has received proper attention so far as painting is concerned are the interior of the tower and exterior of the dwelling.

You are directed to submit any statement you may desire to make, through official channels, within three days from the receipt of this letter. Any statement made must be couched in temperate language, free from countercharges, and confined to the point at issue. If you desire to make no statement, you will so state in writing.[68]

On August 3ʳᵈ, keeper Buckridge responded to the charges, which only made matters worse for him, as it exposed additional problems:

In regards to paper being laid on floor of engine room to absorb the oil, and saturated with oil. It has all ways been my instructions whoever was running the engines to see that these papers and pails and all oils were cleaned up. This has always been my custom since I have been keeper…It was every efficient and neat when I was on Race Rock Light station and a very good idea, but it seems not on this station.

Every joint and connection in the air line leaks oil and papers were put on the floor while the engines were running to keep the oil off the floor. If there was one newspaper in a box with oil on it I did not know it. As to several pairs of overalls, there was one pair that belonged to 1ˢᵗ asst. Miller that I knew about, as I don't own a pair myself. As to the torches being improperly packed and dirty. They were packed the way I was taught and I have been able to get my sirens going in the 10 minutes allowed. As to there being dirty I had them all apart, screens thoroughly washed only a short time ago and they were working good the last time I started the engines.

As to 5 gallon cans with contents, three of them I drew off the 600 gallon tank which was sweating from the vent pipe and I thought that was the proper thing to do to save the oil, and the first time the engines were run it would have been used.

The entire tower was painted and whitewashed inside and out, the tower entrance whitewashed and painted, the engine room doors and windows painted by the middle of May, and the stairs and iron floors in tower twice so far this year, and you must remember there has been 6000 or more people gone up and down those stairs since. If I paint them during the summer it will take three days for them to dry thoroughly as a space has to be left to walk on at one side of the stair…

As to the siren automatic I thought at the time it was the most efficient thing to do to get it working as we have been having long runs of fog, and, as it was, the automatic was running 17 hours 55 minutes before the fog lifted…

Those particular windows in the lantern that are rusty have been scraped and red leaded four times so far this year. The last time the visitors got paint all over them selves after being cautioned, and found a lot of fault about that. I cannot seem to please the public and you at the same time.

I cannot see how I am going to stop the wash and erosion about the lighthouse grounds. I have done a lot of work in regards to it and it washes out the first time it rains, so there is nothing to show for my work. I put 47 wheelbarrow loads of stones and gravel in the roadway by actual count…

I have worked harder on this station than I have ever had to before and as there is not a lazy bone in my body I don't see how I can do more than I am during the summer months. There has been 4027 people in the tower during July and more than 60,000 on the grounds (besides 302 hrs of fog from June 21 to July 20), and looking after them, answering their questions, cleaning up their dirt is no small undertaking.

I have done the best I can and if this letter is not satisfactory I cannot see how I can do more until the summer months are over.[69]

Montauk Point Lighthouse before 1938. Fog signal building at right. Small building in foreground at lower right was the "outhouse." (Queens Borough Public Library Long Island Division, Joseph Burt, Sr. Photographs)

On August 14, 1933 a report to the Commissioner of Lighthouses indicated that keeper Buckridge's explanation:

...offers little or nothing that might be deemed satisfactory when consideration is given to the matter of maintaining the station in an efficient and creditable manner. The conditions found at this station, as well as the keeper's explanations, give ample evidence to show that the proper and efficient maintenance and management of the station is beyond the capabilities of Mr. Buckridge.[70]

The report went on to mention other deficiencies at Montauk Point Light, and, based on keeper Buckridge's apparent inability to maintain the station properly, plans were made to have him transferred and demoted from head keeper at Montauk to 1st assistant keeper at the Orient Point Light Station at the tip of Long Island's North Fork. This action was to take effect on September 1, 1933. His salary would be decreased from $1740 to $1620.[71]

The news must have been very disheartening for Thomas Buckridge, but once word of these events became known to certain influential people who resided on Montauk, letters of support for Buckridge were offered. His immediate neighbor, politician Lathrop Brown, was among those who vouched for his reputation. In a letter to lighthouse commissioner George Putnam from the Administrative Assistant to the Secretary, it was written:

[Brown] claims that he is thoroughly familiar with conditions at the lighthouse and that Buckridge has been a very efficient and capable keeper and that the punishment which it is now proposed be meted out to him in the way of a reduction and transfer is too severe and unfair. Mr. Brown claims that he has seen the previous keeper [John E. Miller] and his son [Jack Miller], who is still an assistant, both intoxicated and in such a condition as not to be able to attend to their duties. He says that Buckridge is a total abstainer and attends strictly to his work; that in his opinion the Department should endeavor to furnish more competent assistants and keep Buckridge at the station.[72]

A letter was sent to Secretary Daniel C. Roper from prominent Montauk resident Perry B. Duryea, which included the signatures of about fifty Montauk protesters. Duryea wrote: "During his term as Keeper at Montauk, Mr. Buckridge has built up an excellent reputation in the Community, being most courteous, honest and efficient. We respectfully request that the reason for his being transferred be reinvestigated and that he be retained as Keeper of Montauk Light House".[73]

Theodore Monell wrote to Commissioner Putnam on October 1, 1933: "I have been coming to Montauk Point since 1912, and... [i]t is my considered judgment that the Lighthouse is more efficiently administered than under the prior administration to a marked degree."[74]

Ambrose O'Connell, Special Assistant to the Postmaster General, added his support on October 2, 1933:

The Chairman of the Suffolk County Democratic Committee has written me of his interest in the case of Thomas A. Buckridge... It is stated that Mr. Buckridge has small children in school and the location of the lighthouse at Orient Point would seriously handicap him. Unless this reassignment is made for disciplinary reasons or inefficiency it is felt that Mr. Buckridge's retention would be most desirable...and sincerely appreciated by his friends.[75]

Windmill on the Lathrop Brown estate in 1923. The property was located immediately west of the lighthouse on the cliffs overlooking the Atlantic Ocean. The estate was broken up for the construction of Camp Hero during World War II. The mill stands today in Wainscott, Long Island. (Queens Borough Public Library,
Long Island Division, Eugene L. Armbruster Collection)

As a result of the outpouring of support for keeper Thomas Buckridge, the case was reviewed by the Lighthouse Service, and on October 13, 1933 a lengthy six-page report was submitted by Lighthouse Service Administrative Assistant W. P. Harman. Excerpts follow:

The keeper's reply of August 3 is rambling in character and is mainly of the confession and avoidance type; it possibly does not do him justice in its explanation of conditions and circumstances...

...it seems proper to take into account the previous record of the keeper and of the station, and the surrounding conditions, as well as the immediate facts and circumstances...

While at Race Rock Station Buckridge's official record was very good, he having been commended four times from 1926 to 1928 for the excellent condition of his station. No record of complaint or criticism is found.

Until a few years ago Montauk Point was very isolated and little visited by the public; and except on the occasions of official inspections conditions there apparently did not promptly or fully come to the attention of the district office. Moreover, the appearance of station and grounds was not of such prime importance. At present, however, there is a concrete state road leading to the reservation, and a state park adjoining, with the result that the lighthouse is visited by several thousand people each year, and the appearance of buildings, grounds, etc., is of greater importance. These conditions necessarily create more work for the keepers...

During the last years of...[John E. Miller's] incumbency he was in poor health and evidently unable fully to perform the required duties, in consequence of which the station appears to have become run down and a laxness in discipline among the keepers to have existed. In addition his official record left much to be desired; it shows one caution and three reprimands for different reasons...

There seems considerable ground for inferring that both the assistant keepers were more or less affected by the standards maintained at the station prior to 1930...

The records indicate that there has been no little friction between keeper Buckridge and assistant keeper Miller; and conditions at the station make it difficult to obtain convincing corroborating evidence as to matters of difference between them. It seems clear that the assistant keeper is one who requires frequent "jacking up", probably due in large measure to habits of work and attitude that he had fallen into during the time his father was keeper.

On the other hand it must be said that Buckridge lacks something as a disciplinarian and a manager of his subordinates. In my investigation, however, I was impressed that he is honest, conscientious, and desires to do his best for the Service and the improvement of his station; also that his position is not an easy one, with the number of buildings and items of equipment and extensive grounds to be kept up, complicated with many visitors during the summer months, and with an assistant keeper apparently lacking in cooperation...

...in view of all the facts in the record and the fact that it is not customary to inflict a severe penalty for a first time offence, it seems difficult to escape the conclusion that the punishment proposed for Keeper Buckridge is unduly severe at this time and that he is entitled to a further chance to make good.[76]

George R. Putnam, Lighthouse Commissioner, in a letter to the Department of Commerce, issued his own verdict on the matter on October 19, 1933:

The Bureau recommends withdrawal of the action of the Department...for the transfer and demotion of Mr. Buckridge. It is considered necessary, however, to issue to Mr. Buckridge a reprimand, with the Department's approval, with respect to the condition of the station under his charge as found by the Superintendent in July last.[77]

Finally, on November 3, 1933, after more than three months since the inflammatory inspection report by Superintendent J. T. Yates, Thomas Buckridge was notified by the Lighthouse Bureau:

...after careful investigation and consideration of your record has decided to give you further opportunity at your present station to correct the conditions on account of which your transfer was heretofore proposed. You are, however, reprimanded on account of the unsatisfactory conditions disclosed in the inspection and cautioned of the necessity of maintaining the station up to the standards required by the Service. The office of the Superintendent will advise you in detail as to the measure to be taken by you to improve the conditions at the station.[78]

Although keeper Buckridge had weathered the political storm, there would be other sub par inspections in the coming years. But it appears the aforementioned considerations again were taken into account. Buckridge remained at Montauk for nearly ten more years.

R. G. Lamb inspected the station on August 17, 1934 and reported a variety of problems, including poor scores in station neatness and cleanliness of the keepers:

Station: Cleanliness 70; Orderliness 80; Operation 80

Personnel:	Neatness	Conduct	Efficiency
Buckridge	70	80	80
Miller	70	80	80
Warrington	70	80	80

Inspector Lamb wrote:

I arrived at 7:00 am. Fog signal house was dirty; about one day's sand and flies. Keeper stated he had been repairing lawn mower. But it had not been thoroughly cleaned thereafter.

Shelves, window sills, etc., covered with dirt and sand. Sirens dripping oil. Kerosene spilled on floor under cock and on floor around engine #1. Service tray greasy. Bottom of oil tanks have rust scale. Paint is on tanks too heavy.

Patch of weeds by tower door to be cut. Window frame in storeroom to be painted and glass reputtied…Gate wide open. Keeper states no one comes in any more. Instructed to keep gate closed.

Garage to be cleaned of old bags. Watchroom gallery rail to be painted. Tower steps need sweeping. Gummed oil on lens clock…

Keeper states that he has no ammonia, soap, sal soda, matches and only one gallon of alcohol. That he needs his supplies to clean with, and will not have enough alcohol to start engines and lamp much longer.

Roof needs renewing. Toilet needed."[79]

MONTAUK POINT LIGHT AND TURTLE COVE, LONG ISLAND, N.Y.

Montauk Point Lighthouse from the north in 1941. (Photo by Bill Keller in the collection of Margaret Buckridge Bock)

Commissioner Putnam addressed the problems to keeper Buckridge, but in a tone noticeably less harsh than that of Superintendent Yates previously:

It appears that conditions at your station are not fully up to the standard that the Bureau expects and requires. This relates in particular to matters affecting cleanliness and orderliness of the station and your rating for personal neatness. The condition of fog signal building and apparatus is a matter of special criticism.

The Bureau requests that you make every effort to remedy and improve these conditions before the next inspection of your station.[80]

Lamb's report brought results, as seen in the next inspection on December 6, 1934, tarnished only by the not surprising absence of assistant keeper Miller:

Station: Cleanliness 85; Orderliness 85, Operation 85		
Personnel: Neatness	Conduct	Efficiency
Buckridge 85	85	85
Miller	not seen	
Warrington 85	85	85[81]

The last inspection report on file in the National Archives was dated May 13, 1935 when inspector Lamb again came to the lighthouse. Ratings continued to be very satisfactory, plus the fact that assistant keeper Miller was present.

Station: Cleanliness 85, Orderliness 85, Operation 85		
Personnel: Neatness	Conduct	Efficiency
Buckridge 85	85	85
Miller 85	85	85
Warrington 85	85	85[82]

In addition to lighthouse inspections by the Lighthouse Bureau, "Recommendation as to Aids to Navigation" forms were occasionally filed which proposed improvements to light stations. Forms on file in the National Archives from 1934-1939 illustrate these changes.

With the great influx of visitors to the Montauk Point Lighthouse in the 1930s, Turtle Hill was taking a beating from the constant flow of footsteps up to the tower. On February 13, 1934 it was proposed by Superintendent J. T. Yates to "construct [a] concrete road and curb, grade the approaching slope to the Lighthouse, install pipe rail fence and gate."

According to Yates, the necessity was "to provide a safe and direct means of approach to tower. The fence is to enclose the buildings and needed property. Grading to be done to stop gullying and eroding of approach slope to light station, and to protect visitors from possible accidents and injury while visiting the station. Estimated cost $4,710.00".

Further comments from Yates: "This station is visited by some 4,000 people monthly during the summer season. The direct and most used approaches to the tower are over a dangerous, steep, badly eroded and gullied slope. It is proposed to grade this slope and construct a concrete road to the tower."[83] This was accomplished later that year.

On March 31, 1938 Superintendent Yates made a proposal for vast improvements at the light station, which amounted to a modernization of the entire facility: "Improve well; install electric pump with running water in dwelling, modernize kitchens, install bathrooms, install sewage disposal system; install electricity. Estimated cost $4,687.50".[84]

The need to improve living conditions in the dwelling was undoubtedly bolstered by existing problems, such as the inadequate water supply. The cistern, constructed in 1860 to collect rain water from roofs on the surrounding structures, could hold 2,717 gallons of water. It was used for a variety of purposes including drinking, though it had to be boiled first.

Tourists visit the Montauk Lighthouse, ca. 1937. Note the Shagwong Reef Range Light on the parapet of the lighthouse tower. (Montauk Library)

In 1935, however, problems with the cistern and other unsanitary conditions on the lighthouse property were brought to the attention of the Suffolk County Department of Health in Riverhead. The county wrote a letter to the Bureau of Lighthouses on November 20th stating that an inspection had been conducted on the property a week earlier, at which time water samples were taken from the cistern and the well. The cistern water was found to be "highly colored and had a disagreeable taste," and though the well was a "considerable distance from the Lighthouse" it was deemed "desirable and advisable that the water supply be obtained in the future" from the well. In addition, the health department directed that the cistern water be boiled before drinking or cooking. A recommendation was made for the well water to be piped to the house.[85]

Jennie Burt poses on running board of a vintage automobile at Montauk Point in 1930. (Queens Borough Public Library, Long Island Division, Joseph Burt Sr. Photographs)

Threatening skies roll in over Montauk Point Lighthouse in this 1930s view. The hurricane of September 21, 1938 brought more than just cloud cover as it caused much destruction to the Montauk Peninsula. (Montauk Point Lighthouse Museum)

It was also found that sink drainage was only about twenty feet from the dwelling. A recommendation was made for the installation of septic tanks, cesspools, or "some other underground method of disposal." The privies were found to be poorly ventilated and the "brick pits are so deep that it is difficult to remove the material." Additional recommendations were made for the installation of modern plumbing with water carriage toilet facilities and a disposal system.[86]

Superintendent Yates responded to the County's concerns on December 14th saying, "There are many stations which still have to depend on cisterns for water supply. I can see no reason why the cistern water at Montauk should be unsuitable for use if keeper exercises proper care in cleaning out and caring for cisterns."[87]

This was followed on December 27th by a letter to the health department from the Lighthouse Bureau's chief engineer, R. R. Tinkham, which stated that improvements at Montauk "have been under consideration for some time but have been deferred due to the urgency of other projects and the inadequacy of the present water supply."[88]

The issue resurfaced in 1937 when New York City judge Meier Steinbrink wrote to the Lighthouse Bureau about the deplorable conditions that existed at Montauk Light:

The only water supply that they have is from a well, which is about 150 feet from the house…They have no running water in the house and therefore no provision whatever for hot water.…Speaking from a long-time experience with real estate matters…I know that it would be a very simple matter and not at all expensive to pipe the house and connect with the well water, installing an instantaneous hot water heater, which would likewise furnish the occupants with a supply of hot water.[89]

Commissioner of Lighthouses, H. D. King responded on December 2nd: "It has for many years been the policy of this Service to improve living conditions of keepers at light stations as rapidly as practicable within the limit of available funds. The dwellings are in many cases old and poorly adapted to such improvements, because of which fact and also because of their isolation in many cases, the work has been more difficult and expensive than would be usual." [90]

Superintendent J. T. Yates responded on December 6th: "The Bureau's attention is called to the fact that the water supply at this station is from cisterns. Water is available in each Keeper's kitchen from a pump. The well is just an additional supply, and not the only source. The well has been filled in with sand and must be improved before it can be piped to the house. This matter has been investigated and when funds are available, this work will be accomplished.[91]

Ten months later the Great Hurricane of 1938 damaged the light station. Jonathan Miller, then a young man of 14, spoke in a 2007 interview of the experience:

There was no forecast of any storm, except being one of those typical September days; started out nice. Around 2:00 or 3:00 teachers decided to move us away from windows because the building at that time had slate on it and the wind was blowing hard enough to blow all of those off. During the height of the storm we took a peek out the back door and we could see where the ocean and Fort Pond Bay had come together down in the fishing village. Some of the kids had families down that way.

My folks were worried because they had seen the bus go out to pick us up at school by 3:00-3:30pm. Meanwhile, the storm was getting worse and worse. When the storm was over we didn't go home that night. Different families that lived in the area around the school within walking distance put us up for the night. I don't recall the name of the family we stayed with. Their father was unable to get home that night due to the washout of the railroad at Hither Hills. We spent the night with his wife and two children and went home next day.

At the light my folks and the Warringtons got inside the base of the light when the storm hit. The storm blew a lot of shingles off the dwelling itself and, I believe, toppled one of the chimneys. It was fierce enough and they had concerns for their safety, so they went into the bottom of the lighthouse because they knew the tower's thick walls wouldn't bring harm to anybody.

The Red Cross was in the village taking care of people for a long time and we didn't return to school for days. There were people that had homes and were now displaced.

On October 14, 1938, about three weeks after the devastating storm, Superintendent Yates proposed repairs: "During the storm of Sept. 21, 1938, the shingle roofs of all the buildings on Montauk Point were so badly torn and ripped that it is considered more economical to remove the roofs' covering and recover them than to attempt to repair and have a continuous trouble with leaks... Estimate cost @ $2,197."[92]

Proposals were sent to more than thirty companies for the modernization of the station. The winning bidder, C. J. Marino, described the scope of the work:

Entire work of relathing and replastering three bathrooms and tower hall, erecting partition across tower hall, etc.; installing running water in dwelling, modernizing kitchens and bathrooms and sewage disposal system; installing wiring and outlets for electric current; removing and renewing roof covering of dwelling, ells to tower, porch, fog signal house and garage, patching plaster in dwelling, and other repairs to buildings at Montauk Point Light Station, Montauk, Long Island, New York....$4989.60.[93]

The improvements were made later that year.

On October 28, 1938, Yates proposed the relocation of the Shagwong Reef range light, which was severely damaged in the hurricane. He stated: "It is proposed to move the lamp and lens into the main lantern, and install a low pedestal therefor [sic], and remove the house on the gallery. The elevation of the light will be changed from 161 feet above water to 165 feet above water."[94]

Shortly after the New Year in 1939, Yates recommended a concrete road be constructed from the existing road up Turtle Hill to the garage at the light station. The wooden garage floor, he noted, was "badly eaten away by termites." To eliminate this problem and do away with the unused garage cellar, he proposed filling in the cellar with dirt and installing a concrete floor. The estimated cost was $1627.50.[95] Bids were received from more than two dozen firms, with Simon E. Hunt the winner at $1800. The work was completed later that year.

The installation of a radiobeacon at the Montauk Point Light Station was proposed by Yates on May 20, 1939 "to assist shipping in vicinity of Montauk."[96] It was installed in September 1940.

Shipwrecks

During the Buckridge era at Montauk Point Light, several shipwrecks occurred in the vicinity of the lighthouse property. The *Comanche* came ashore at the lighthouse on January 4, 1931; the Canadian rum-runner *Algie* on February 20, 1931;

the 189-foot tanker *Raritan Sun* on July 14, 1935; the fishing schooner *Julia A* on November 13, 1935; and the *Mary P. Mosquito* on November 26, 1936.[97]

According to Bucky Bock, "the most exciting one was the *Comanche* which came ashore right at the Point with a group of party fisherman. Fortunately, no lives were lost. We made coffee and sandwiches for them, and some of them came into the house to 'dry out', since they were all slightly inebriated."

The *Raritan Sun* was another wreck Bucky remembered, "halfway between us and the Coast Guard Station [at Ditch Plains] and I remember walking down to it, but the Coast Guard really took care of it."

The tanker had left Marcus Hook, south of Philadelphia and headed for Phillipsdale, Rhode Island, carrying several hundred gallons of petroleum. In a letter to the lighthouse superintendent, keeper Buckridge wrote: "The tanker *Raritan Sun* is ashore about 3 miles southwest of station. She grounded at about 4:30 pm in thick fog, which came with southerly wind. Second Assistant Warrington on watch. He had the fog signal going about 4:10 pm, as soon as we could see any indication of fog from here. The tanker hails from Philadelphia. There is considerable complaint that the sirens cannot be heard to the southwest when there is any wind at all from that direction."[98]

The *Comanche* ran aground at Montauk Point on January 4, 1931. The crew "dried out" at the lighthouse. (Margaret Buckridge Bock)

The *Raritan Sun* carried a cargo of petroleum, which as a result of the grounding, began escaping through a large gash. The crew of ten was rescued without incident. There were concerns that the oil in the ocean would have an adverse effect on local fishing for the season, but it soon cleared away.[99]

J. T. Yates responded on July 20, 1935 to the Commissioner of Lighthouses about a possible cause of the wreck: "The horns…are not properly placed so as to give best results to the greater part of the traffic approaching this light station, for the greater part of the traffic approaches from a northerly or southerly direction."[100]

The vessel was safely refloated on July 20th and taken towards New London.

The 80-foot trawler, *Julia A,* was bound from New England to the Fulton Market in New York City in November 1935 when it ran aground west of the lighthouse in a heavy fog. Its captain Eric Beso, was taken from the boat by members of the Ditch Plains Coast Guard Station and the *Julia A's* crew of three came ashore in a dory. Aid came from two cutters sent from the Coast Guard base at New London. The *Julia A*, which contained some 40,000 pounds of haddock, was later refloated.[101]

Lighthouse Visitors

Of course, the lighthouse was not without visitors, some of whom spent hours making the drive to Long Island's eastern tip to enjoy the splendor of Montauk Point and its majestic lighthouse. During the mid 1930s, an average of 4,500 visitors came in July and as many as 7,000 in August. Keeper Thomas Buckridge found himself being interviewed by the press about twice a year but claimed he "practically never recognizes any statement in the interview as his own."[102]

Generally, the light tower was open to the public every day except Sunday from 10:00a.m. until noon and 1:00-3:00p.m.. It was the responsibility of the keeper on duty to escort groups up and down the tower stairs. When it became busy in summer, one keeper would remain at the base of the tower and another would stay in the lantern, letting groups up at intervals. (This practice continues today at the Lighthouse Museum.) In the winter, there were fewer visitors and the keepers made about three to five trips up the tower per day.

Bucky Bock felt that the number of visitors increased as a result of the opening of the Montauk Point State Park in 1927, plus the start of the fishermen trains from New York City. She said that sometimes visitors "were fun and broke the monotony of our semi-isolation. At other times they were pains in the neck. Some of them tried to rip shingles off the house for souvenirs. One time, when we were all in the kitchen, we could hear someone playing the piano in our living room. They were quite indignant when told that these were private quarters. We tried to keep the screen door locked in the summer for this reason. We also got a big laugh when we overheard a man explaining about the docks (fishing piers). He said, 'Oh, that's where they land their supplies in winter.' Since the pier stood in a foot of water, he must have thought the winter tides were really high."[103] [The piers were constructed annually by local fishermen for many years in the 1920s and 1930s.]

Thomas Buckridge patiently awaiting another group of tourists at the Montauk Point Lighthouse,1939. (Margaret Buckridge Bock)

Bucky explained that the presence of visitors interfered with the daily work of the keepers: "If they were painting at 10:00a.m. they had to stop and put on their uniforms. They couldn't take visitors up in their work clothes. They had to be in full uniform to do that. In summer they had to have their jacket on. There were no summer uniforms. Regulations didn't say the lighthouse had to be open on Sundays. Tourism was not the chief thing at the lighthouse. It was an incidental. Visitors would sometimes make things dirty, drop papers, all of which had to be picked up."

Visitors hike up Turtle Hill to tour the lighthouse in this postcard view, 1937. (Queens Borough Public Library, Long Island Division, Postcard Collection)

Despite the growing numbers of tourists each year and the time required to escort them, the keepers diligently continued to greet visitors and take them up the tower. By 1939 the near-constant presence of the public was wearing on the lighthouse crew, as evidenced by assistant keeper George Warrington's comment: "So long as they don't get noisy, we don't pay any attention to them".[104]

With such a huge influx of visitors, there was talk of making the Montauk Point Light Station a "show station," calling for the dwelling to be modernized. However, on July 22, 1930 Superintendent J. T. Yates stated that certain repairs would be made at Montauk, but "no funds will be expended to create a show station at this or other points until more important work is cared for." He added: "The installation of a public toilet is not contemplated".[105]

On April 2, 1937 Yates wrote to the Lighthouse Bureau of the effect that the great volume of visitors was having on the keepers at Montauk:

The Bureau is advised that due primarily to the development of a State Park in the vicinity of Montauk Point Light Station...the number of visitors has increased to a point that during the Summer months it takes practically all of the time of the keepers to take care of visitors and police the grounds, with the result that they are unable to perform but little station maintenance work...It is proposed to employ two Laborers, with pay at the rate of $5.12 per diem, during the months of June, July and August.[106]

**Thomas and Sarah Buckridge provide a warm welcome at the Montauk
Lighthouse, ca. 1938. (Margaret Buckridge Bock)**

The Lighthouse Bureau responded on April 16th giving approval for the laborers but noting the rate of pay would be allowed only if "it is not in excess of the rate paid locally for this class of employment." In addition, the Bureau made a point of defining the type of visitors that should be permitted, stating that it would be "practical [to] deny admission to the reservation to persons in bathing suits, insisting as a matter of ordinary procedure that they be properly clad as a prerequisite to admittance".[107]

In a liberal tone, Superintendent Yates replied that it would be:

...contrary to the best interests of the Service to endeavor to limit parties visiting the lighthouse station...to any stipulated hours...or to place the visitors under the escort of the Keepers, for they are far too numerous around the grounds...

The only restriction which is considered desirable is the limiting of the visiting hours for visiting the tower and the buildings. This office can also see no justification in making an attempt to deny admission to the light station reservation to persons wearing bathing suits, for there is no restriction on such clothing in [Montauk Point State] Park itself.[108]

A sense of the extent of public visitation at Montauk Point Lighthouse was noted in 1937 by Meade C. Dobson, Managing Director of the Long Island Association. He reported a record 18,547 visitors that year, but pointed out that "the count is, however, made only of those who enter the lighthouse tower and does not include ten times as many more who visit the Point. It is estimated that considerably more than 100,000 people have already visited Montauk this summer [of 1939]."[109]

Thomas Buckridge attributed high visitor numbers in 1939 to the pleasant weather and the station's proximity to the World's Fair in New York City.[110]

Thomas Buckridge enjoying the warm weather at the top of Montauk Lighthouse, August 27, 1936. Note the young visitor at left. (Margaret Buckridge Bock)

World War II

On July 1, 1939, shortly before the outbreak of World War II, the Lighthouse Service was absorbed into the U. S. Coast Guard. Montauk Point Light Station, which had been part of the Third Lighthouse District, now became part of the New York Coast Guard District headquartered in New York City.

Civilian lightkeepers were given the opportunity to join the Coast Guard at ranks commensurate with their duties, years of experience, and service record. Sixty-five-year-old Thomas Buckridge did not join because of his age. Jack Miller was recommended for the rank of petty officer 1st class, "in view of poor service record." He rejected the offer and completed his service at Montauk as a civilian.

George Warrington sought a transfer to the new service. As part of his preparation, he wrote to the Coast Guard asking if the prescribed uniform for lightkeepers should be "a surfman's uniform or the regulation sailor's uniform."[111] The reply soon came back to wear the sailor's uniform.[112]

In July 1941 Warrington reported to the Coast Guard base at New London, Connecticut for a physical. He continued working at the lighthouse as a civilian until August 21, 1942 when he officially resigned from the Lighthouse Service; the following day he was accepted into the Coast Guard as a boatswain's mate 2nd class and resumed his lighthouse duties.[113] His Lighthouse Service salary of $1,620 (less $240 for rent), continued in the Coast Guard until his retirement in 1943.

The late 1930s saw the rise of Nazi Germany and its allies, Italy and Japan. War began with Germany's invasion of Poland on September 1, 1939. The United States responded by heightening security along its coastlines. According to Bucky Bock:

As the war clouds gathered, the Coast Guard from Ditch Plains used to walk the beach to the lighthouse. Later, the coast guardsmen from Ditch Plains would work a shift at the lighthouse. I thus became acquainted with quite a few of the younger ones. My friends were always eager to visit Montauk with me, and I would call on the Coast Guard telephone to let them know I was around. Incidentally, this was our only telephone- an old-fashioned type with a handle to turn. I was able to call home once or twice from East Hampton by going to the Coast Guard station there. When war was declared, the Coast Guard took over the Lighthouse Service, which had formerly been under the Department of the Treasury. The family quarters at Montauk were discontinued and mother went to Amagansett to stay with Bessie Parsons. Later, she returned to Connecticut to our house in Essex. Dad...was too old to be inducted into the Coast Guard. He continued working as a lighthouse keeper, but as a civilian, until he retired."[114]

Jonathan Miller said of the war years:

My cousin Milton (born November 17, 1914) was assigned to the Ditch Plain Coast Guard Station. Just before the war they had a watch station at the lighthouse. A truck brought the men out every four hours for a changing of the guard. Milton was one of several Coastguardsmen. They were sheltered in the engine room most of the time they were there. Out on the bank they had a watchman's clock. It had a special key with a number on the clock. They had to punch this clock to show they had been there. It was quite a ways out on the bank overlooking the ocean. The men were out there mainly for ships in distress. There were quite a few fishing fleets and charter boats that came from Lake Montauk and Fort Pond Bay."

Surveillance tower at the Ditch Plains Coast Guard Station, Montauk, March 1941. (Margaret Buckridge Bock)

Concurrent with war in Europe, the Montauk Point Lighthouse entered the modern era with the installation of a 1000-watt incandescent electric bulb on July 1, 1940. It sent a beam of light 19 nautical miles (22 statute miles) out to sea. At the same time the Shagwong Reef range light was removed from the lantern. Two months later, a radio beacon was activated at the station to aid vessels plying Long Island Sound. Also, emergency generators were installed at the station in the event of a total power failure.

As the war intensified, many light stations were taken over by the military. Beginning in 1941, the Montauk Light gradually became part of the Eastern Coast Defense Shield. A log entry for June 7th of that year stated: "Coast artillery practically in charge," and on June 9th, "Army occupying everything."

Construction of the artillery fire tower (in camouflage, right of lighthouse) by the U. S. Army in 1942 presented an ominous appearance in this ca. 1943 view. The U.S. Army had begun occupation of the lighthouse property in 1941 as part of the Eastern Coast Defense Shield. Artillery fire was coordinated with Camp Hero just to the west of the lighthouse property. (Montauk Point Lighthouse Museum)

Two days after the attack on Pearl Harbor on December 7, 1941, the assignment of "Standing air plane watch" was entered in the light station log. Coast Guard personnel began standing double watches in 1942 with assistance from the civilian keepers.

Lighthouse keepers and Coast Guard personnel appear ready for an inspection in 1942. Standing are Keeper Thomas Buckridge (second from left), Jack Miller (third from left), and George Warrington (far right). (Arthur Dunne Collection)

Unfortunately, the beacon in the light tower silhouetted allied vessels as they sailed by Montauk Point, making them easy targets for enemy submarines. To solve the problem, the 1000-watt bulb was replaced by a 100-watt bulb on August 14, 1942. For the duration of the war the lighthouse was used more for surveillance than for navigation.

The last wartime log entry by the lightkeepers was made on April 30, 1943. It indicated that the military was in full control of the Montauk Point Light Station. Keeper Thomas Buckridge had departed on January 27th. George Warrington was present as a boatswains mate 2nd class, having joined the Coast Guard, and John (Jack) Miller as a civilian keeper.

During 1943, the Artillery Fire Control Tower was constructed a short distance east of the lighthouse. It was here that artillery fire was coordinated with the 16-inch guns located at Camp Hero just west of the lighthouse property. Covered with camouflage paint, the tower was used to survey the surrounding waters for the presence of German submarines. Camp Hero was established as a military base but was designed to resemble a quaint New England fishing village from the air. It occupied lands that included the former Lathrop Brown estate and the Wyandanee Inn. As many as 600 servicemen occupied the site during the war years.

Above--One of the powerful guns at fortified Camp Hero, ready to defend Montauk and eastern Long Island, ca. 1943. (Montauk Point Lighthouse Museum)

Below-- Margaret Buckridge, left, and friends by the kitchen entrance to keeper's dwelling at Montauk Lighthouse, August 1941. Note the radio beacon tower at rear and the new Montauk Point State Parkway in the distance. (Margaret Buckridge Bock)

From an interview with former Staff Sergeant Arthur (Art) M. Dunne in August 2008 at his home in Amagansett, Long Island we get a sense of the military presence at Montauk Point during World War II. With a twinkle in his eye and wonderful sense of humor, the 92-year old veteran spoke freely about his life experiences. Born in Enfield, Connecticut on February 5, 1916, he spent his early years on the family farm in that town. Art experienced far more dangerous situations in his life <u>before</u> he entered the U. S. Army than during his active duty years. For example, he was struck by lightning twice.

As he put it, "You know how they say lightning never strikes twice in the same place? Well, that's a lot of crap!"

The first time Art was struck, he was working in a hayfield: "A storm came up. I decided to run for the house when lightning hit the pitchfork I was carrying and cut it right in half. Didn't knock me out but it scared the holy hell out of me!"

His second experience with lightning also was at the farm: "We used to play baseball between the two tobacco sheds. There was a big tree nearby that seemed to get hit every time there was a storm. When the storm came, the others were going under the barbed wire fence to get away. I cut a hole in the fence to help them and the lightning hit the big tree and traveled to the fence and it froze me! The guy with me took the baseball bat and smashed the wire, breaking the connection. I was out for a couple of minutes."

Another time when Art was home on leave from the service, he was gored by the family's pet bull, breaking six of his ribs. Normally somewhat playful, the bull's attack was almost fatal, but Art survived: "When I returned to duty, my buddies didn't believe me when I told them what happened. They probably thought I'd done it."

While living at Enfield he met Mary Frances O'Connor (born September 20, 1918), who lived about fifteen miles north in Chicopee, Massachusetts. They were married on June 20, 1942.

Art's "number" was called early in the first peacetime draft in October of 1940 and on February 15, 1941 he found himself stationed at Fort Terry on Plum Island, New York as part of the 242nd Coast Artillery. He worked in the control tower with another soldier named Eddie Resnick. They had a brush with danger the first night.

When we first arrived there was no room for us to sleep so they put us up inside a mine store house for the night. The sergeant said though there was no heat at least it was shelter. Once inside we noticed what looked like a lot of small beer kegs. We rolled them out and used them for pillows. The next morning the captain shouted, "Everybody out! Immediately!" Those pillows turned out to be land mines that had never been deactivated. And there we were rolling them around! We never knew what the hell they were!

In July 1942 Art and Eddie were transferred to the Montauk Point Light Station, a month after the landing of the German saboteurs at Amagansett. Art had attained the rank of staff sergeant. His assignment was to install and operate a radar station, which at that time may well have been the first of its kind along the entire east coast of the country.

When he arrived at Montauk, he, Eddie, and others lived in a couple of tents that stood just south of the garage at the foot of Turtle Hill below the lighthouse. During that first year Art remembered: "Believe me, we slept with all our clothes on and all the blankets we could get. We were only allowed fifty gallons of oil a month and we were always freezing! Marshall Prado [who operated a gas station in Montauk] would give us many a 50-gallon drum of oil for free, with the stipulation that we pick it up ourselves. So I rigged up a jeep with a pair of ramps to roll the oil drum on and off."

Pictured left are the tents where Art Dunne and Eddie Resnick slept when they first came to Montauk in 1942. Below are the same tents converted into barracks in 1942 by Art Dunne. Plywood was supplied from Camp Hero.
(Arthur Dunne Collection)

During 1942 at Montauk Point Light Station, the roughly twelve men assigned there were only permitted thirty-three cents a day for rations. They "shot deer, stole potatoes, and accepted provisions from old-timers to get by." [115]

After an uncomfortable year in the tents, Art said:

Captain Henry from Camp Hero gave me a lot of used plywood, 2 x 4's, and old windows. I took them and converted the tents into barracks in 1943. [Lighthouse keeper] Captain [Thomas] Buckridge gave me a set of tools to work with when I built the barracks. He told me they were in the attic of the house and I would have to climb a ladder to get them for myself. When I went in the attic for the tool box I also found two beautiful brass Coast Guard lamps. I asked Captain Buckridge about them. He told me,"Hell, if you want 'em, take 'em." I took 'em.

The lamps are still in the possession of the Dunne family.

Montauk Point Lighthouse, as it appeared in August 1942. Keeper Thomas Buckridge is standing on porch. (Arthur Dunne Collection)

Above--This small lookout shack was situated east of the lighthouse in 1942. The top floor was used to observe aircraft activity. The lower floor was for observing ships and submarine movements. (Arthur Dunne Collection)

Right--A radar tower was constructed in 1943. Built on the site of the lookout shack pictured above, it housed equipment for Seacoast Artillery radar and LORAN. (Arthur Dunne Collection)

Art spoke favorably about the three lighthouse keepers at the Montauk Light: "Buckridge was all right. Very distant. Very strict. There was a big room in the house that had a ping pong table, dominos and some books. No radio or cards or alcohol and he meant it! He was strict as could be but very fair."

"Just don't cross him!" he added, with a laugh.

Art pointed out a picture (previous page) of Buckridge standing in casual clothes on the front porch of the keeper's dwelling: "From here, he would place a peach basket a distance away, stand on the porch with a fishing line and bet anyone 25 cents that he could land the line in the basket. He won a lot of quarters!"

When the photo was later shown to Buckridge's daughter Bucky, she said, "I didn't know about the peach basket story but I am sure he could do it, as he was a great fisherman."

She was surprised to see him out of uniform: "The inspectors would have hated that picture of him in casual clothes. They thought the keepers should be in immaculate uniform at all times, even when doing maintenance work."

"[Jack] Miller was a good guy," continued Art. "So was George Warrington. They both lived up in Springs near East Hampton. There was just the three of them there plus the cook when I came. The cook was a full-blooded Indian from Iowa. The families weren't with them at the time."

By the time the three lighthouse keepers left Montauk in early 1943, the radar tower was under construction, as was the large barracks in the meadow southwest of the lighthouse. Unfortunately, the two structures Art had built were demolished during this time. Awaiting completion of the new barracks, Art moved into a room in Jack Miller's old apartment on the second floor of the lighthouse keeper's dwelling. His handiwork was evident there, when he built a mailbox adjacent to the south main entrance door with compartments for outgoing mail for the Army and the Coast Guard.

"There used to be a public telephone at the entrance to the lighthouse tower," Art said. "I had a desk there with a short wave radio and a 'hot line' and a public line. On the big wall was a huge map of our area. I did my reporting from there for years. Every morning at 11:00, I had to place a call reporting in."

When Camp Hero was under construction, Art became involved there, too. "Captain Henry came to me and said, 'I wish you guys would help us keep an eye out for saboteurs coming up through Turtle Cove and help us with construction.' So we went and we lived like kings. They had food you wouldn't believe. Always at the end we would get a double order of ice cream. We sometimes would go there on Sunday afternoons for dances and dine at the mess hall."

During the war years, Coast Guardsmen from the Ditch Plains Station patrolled the beaches. According to Art, "They would stop in our barracks around midnight and we would give them a cup of coffee and ham sandwiches. They were thrilled over that."

Completed in 1943, the radar tower appears to cast a somber eye over the waters off Montauk Point. The fog signal was moved away from the tower since when it sounded, it interfered with radar signals. (Arthur Dunne Collection)

At the top of Turtle Hill, just east of the lighthouse tower was constructed a small two story wooden lookout shack. Telescopes were used here before the days of radar. According to Art, the person stationed in the top floor surveyed the skies for enemy aircraft, while the person in the lower level scanned the ocean for enemy ships and submarine activity. The shack actually stood on the very spot that the radar tower was constructed upon in 1943.

Art said that the radar tower was built in separate sections, each of which was raised up with a crane and lowered down one on top of the other. The installation of steel rods strengthened the fortification. Inside the tower was contained highly sensitive equipment, including Seacoast Artillery microwave radar, known as SCXR-582, used for harbor patrol and detection of surface craft and low-flying planes. In addition, the radio navigation system known as LORAN (LOng Range Aid to Navigation) was located here. According to Art, the IFF system (Identification Friend or Foe) was used here and PQI enlarged one hundred feet of the baseline for the 16-inch guns in place at neighboring Camp Hero.

Left--Staff Sergeant Arthur Dunne is shown "blowing his own horn" inside the fog signal trumpet at Montauk Point, 1943.

Below—The barracks at Montauk Point in 1943 was near the beach. The facility could accommodate about 30 military personnel.

(Arthur Dunne Collection)

The fog signal had an adverse effect on the radar tower. Art noted: "In June of 1943 that fog horn blew for thirty-one days without stopping. They had to move the horns further away from the radar tower because when they blew they affected radar readings." (His wife Mary joked, "And you wonder why he's deaf now!")

Art was quick to point out the highly secretive nature of his work at Montauk Point: "Our unit was completely separate from the military at Camp Hero. As a matter of fact, there was no record of me even being out there at all! The radar operation was top secret."

In fact, Montauk Point was considered such an important radar station that the standing orders were to self-destruct in the event of an enemy land attack.

"I always wondered whether I'd do it," mused Art in a 1977 interview for the *East Hampton Star*.[116]

The huge 16-inch guns installed in the batteries at Camp Hero were transported to Montauk Point by railroad. Art told of a frightening incident with the guns, given the highly secretive nature of the site:

> *One day when I was getting my hair cut, the guy says to me, "Hey sarge, you know when you were on your short wave radio talking to Fort Wright* [on Fisher's Island, New York], *I heard you on my telephone. I know about the guns coming out." I said, "You gotta be kidding." He says, "No, no, I'm serious! I know the date they're coming."*

Art said the fear was that saboteurs would attempt to dynamite the railroad bridge across the Shinnecock Canal near Hampton Bays, Long Island. At the scheduled time and date, guards were posted at the railroad bridge (about 35 miles west of Montauk Point) to ensure the safe passage of the equipment.

Art added, "Of course, after that they changed my radio frequency since it was very close to telephone frequency. If the weather was right my frequency could've combined with the telephone frequency and anyone could've heard me talking!"

Among Art's responsibilities was to monitor the thousands of ships that passed Montauk Point. This was done via blinker lights from Fort Terry on Plum Island.

"I communicated with an awful lot of them at night," Art remembered. "Used to ask the same four questions: What ship? What nation? What cargo? What port?"

During the war years at Montauk, Art noted there was very little traffic on Long Island's east end, from Riverhead out to Montauk Point. Few people came out to see the lighthouse in those days. That would change drastically following the war, as Montauk became popular with vacationers and more people moved to the eastern tip of Long Island.

War changes the look of a place. The Montauk Point Light Station in 1943, no longer presented the friendly, welcoming appearance of the 1930s. (Arthur Dunne Collection)

Chapter 4

End of an Era

He trimmed the wicks, struck the match, and spent much of his time sitting by a window watching for ships in distress, reading into the deep hours of night, or making ships in bottles. Few keepers fit this quixotic ideal, but it is the one we cherish.

Elinor DeWire
Lighthouses of the Mid-Atlantic Coast

The lightkeepers at Montauk Point Light in the 1930s may not have realized at the time that a new chapter in the station's long history was about to begin. Modernization was the buzzword as the Coast Guard assumed control of lighthouses. Automation was just over the horizon, and sweeping changes lay ahead for Montauk Point. In a slow procession, longtime residents of the lighthouse departed and Coast Guard personnel took over the work. Ultimately, even they would leave.

Bucky Bock left Montauk in February of 1938 and entered nursing school at Hartford Hospital in Connecticut. She returned to Montauk for her sister Elizabeth's wedding on May 15, 1938. Elizabeth married Albert Santi (1912-1995) of Ivoryton, Connecticut. The ceremony was performed in the front parlor of the Buckridge quarters at Montauk Point Light Station by the Reverend John Gordon of the Montauk Community Church. Bucky recalled: "It was not an elaborate ceremony, but it was special to all of us because it took place in the lighthouse".

According to Bucky: "Just the family came. Albert's brother was best man and I was bridesmaid. The Millers and Warringtons were not there. We [the three families] were not social." She said of the celebration: "No champagne or anything like that. Not in my father's lighthouse. He never allowed drinking of any sort."[117]

Not long after this, electricity was installed at the lighthouse, providing the modern conveniences of lighting, heating, and indoor plumbing. When Bucky came back to visit she noted, "my overnight hostesses always offered me the use of their bath tub, which I gratefully accepted...Before that, washing our hair was always a two person task. After all, how could you rinse your hair thoroughly when you had to do so by pouring water from a pitcher?"[118]

Bucky Bock graduated from the Hartford Hospital School of Nursing on June 12, 1941. Afterwards:

I went to the Hartford Visiting Nurses Association and I worked there for about a year and a half. Then I got married and asked for a leave of absence so I could join Bob in Texas but they wouldn't give me one. They asked me if I was going to be a 'camp follower' because I was married! So when he went overseas I didn't want to go back and work for the VNA after that so I got a job at Hamilton Standard as a nurse and after Bob got home we moved to Rocky Hill, Connecticut. I got a job as a school nurse after the children were all in school. While I was there the teachers kept sending all these kids to me with speech problems. So I went back to school and got my bachelo'rs degree and my master's degree in speech therapy. That's now I ended up as being a speech and language pathologist."

After Elizabeth left Montauk and after her children were grown, she worked for Sparre Insurance Agency in Essex, Connecticut. Her husband Albert, known as "Lob," was postmaster in Ivoryton, Connecticut and they lived on Bushy Hill Road. Upon retirement, they relocated to Marietta, Georgia to be near their daughter. Elizabeth died in Roswell, Georgia on June 24, 2004 at the age of ninety-one.

On February 4, 1943, Thomas Buckridge was officially transferred to the Old Saybrook Breakwater Light (also known as the "Outer Light") at the entrance to the Connecticut River. This station was not equipped to accommodate families, so Thomas' wife, Sarah, lived at the family home in Essex and was able to see her husband only a few days every month. His last day of duty at Old Saybrook Light was November 24, 1943. He retired shortly thereafter on January 31, 1944 at the age of seventy. Although the lighthouse service had been absorbed by the Coast Guard in 1939, Thomas Buckridge, because of his advanced age, served out his last days of lighthouse duty as a civilian.

Bucky Bock described the tight quarters at Old Saybrook Light: "The keeper's rooms were right in the tower itself. The first floor was the service room, then the kitchen, bedroom, then the light. There were just two men that lived there; no families. My father was only there a year and a half before he retired at age 70."

Thomas and Sarah Buckridge celebrated their 50th wedding anniversary in March 1951. He died in Essex on August 1, 1955 at the age of eighty-one. Sarah also died at Essex, on August 4, 1962 at the age of eighty-six. Both are buried in Cypress Cemetery at Westbrook, Connecticut.

Bucky Bock and her husband Bob celebrated their 50th anniversary on August 7, 1993. He passed away in December 2006. Today, Bucky continues to live in the historic homestead in Westbrook. Her daughter lives in Hartford.

Jack Miller was listed as a "keeper" at Montauk Point Light when he retired on July 31, 1943, by that time sharing responsibilities with wartime Coast Guard personnel. Miller ended up serving over twenty-five years at Montauk Point Lighthouse. He died in Unadilla, New York on December 1, 1969 at the age of seventy-eight. At the time of his death, he had been a member of the American Legion for forty-three years. He was buried in the Green River Cemetery in Springs, New York.[119] His wife, Maude, predeceased him on January 2, 1966.

Like Miller, George Warrington shared duties and responsibilities with the Coast Guard at Montauk Point Light for some years after the July 1939 consolidation. He left the station early in 1943 and moved to East Hampton, New York in 1944.

Warrington had two sisters, Mary and Virginia, and four brothers, William, John, Abisha, and Manean. His daughter Louise married David Raynor and lived in Nyack, New York. George Warrington, Jr. became a minister and lived in Minerva, Ohio.

Jonathan Miller described the Warrington family in 2007:

> *George retired to East Hampton shortly after leaving the lighthouse. He had a garage there for a time and died not too long after. His widow went back to Delaware to live with her brother.*
>
> *His son, George III, went into the air force during World War II. After he got out he became a minister. He began doing missionary work with the Indians down in Oklahoma. I believe he may have had a church in Maryland somewhere. When we lived at the lighthouse, the minister at the Presbyterian church in Montauk was a young fellow fresh out of the seminary. He and his wife took a real interest in the young people. He would use his own transportation to come out and get us for special occasions. He had a boys and girls club in Montauk and would take us on trips to New York to Grant's Tomb, St John the Divine Church and other places.*
>
> *The Warringtons were- at least Mrs. Warrington was- fairly religious people, but I don't think Mr. Warrington was. George III got the interest from his mother because of the work she did with the minister John Gordon [pastor at Montauk 1937-1943]. George's sister Louise married a minister herself but I'm not sure where she ended up.*

George Warrington's family had settled in the Shepherd's Neck section of Montauk, and when he retired from the service he planned to move to East Hampton. Art Dunne made arrangements to help him move. Warrington died in East Hampton on February 10, 1955, age fifty-three from a heart attack suffered some weeks earlier. He was buried in the Odd Fellows Cemetery in Cumberland, Maryland.[120] He had been a member of East Hampton Town Post 419 of the American Legion.

By 1946, a year after the conclusion of World War II, the Montauk Lighthouse was completely under the control of the Coast Guard. The courageous, exciting, and at times tedious era of the civilian lightkeeper had come to an end. The years of Coast Guard operation (until 1987) would appear mundane in comparison to the now-legendary adventures of the early civilian keepers and their families.

During the Coast Guard era, tourists continued to visit Montauk Point State Park and view the old lighthouse, though during the Cold War years the property often was not accessible to the public.

Margaret Buckridge Bock and her husband, Bob, pose at Montauk Point Lighthouse during the lighthouse bicentennial celebration, June 1, 1996. (Margaret Buckridge Bock)

The ever-present problem of erosion accelerated and threatened the station's very existence. Apathy toward preservation of lighthouses in these years contributed to the loss of numerous historic sites, as did automation and subsequent vandalism, demolition of obsolete stations, and destruction by natural causes. Montauk Lighthouse, without an effective plan to halt the relentless onslaught of erosion on the bluffs of Turtle Hill, seemed doomed.

Then, in 1969, Giorginia Reid (1908-2001), a professional photographer and textile designer, persuaded the Coast Guard to allow her and a group of volunteers to shore up the bluffs surrounding the lighthouse property. Her unique method of terracing with plants had held back the sea at her home, and she was certain it would work at Montauk Point. She began work in April of 1970 at the age of sixty-one and championed the erosion control project for the next sixteen years. Then, from 1986 to 1998 the project was lead by the zealous efforts of Montauk landscaper Greg Donohue, the Montauk Historical Society, and other agencies. Thanks to these people and their dedicated work, the erosion of the bluffs below the lighthouse was virtually halted.

Montauk Point Lighthouse was automated on February 3, 1987. The light and fog signal were mechanized to run self-sufficiently, and the resident Coast Guard crew was notified of impending transfer. To prevent the abandonment of the station, the Montauk Historical Society stepped in almost immediately, and by spring the Montauk Point Lighthouse Museum was opened. It continues to welcome visitors to this day.

In a presentation she gave at Old Saybrook in 1991, Bucky Bock spoke of her lighthouse experiences: "Although I have visited many other facilities, visiting them and living in one are a totally different experience. I am very happy to have had this opportunity in my past and I certainly loved every moment of it."[121]

When asked in an interview in July 2007 if she missed Montauk after so many years, Bucky replied: "I did at first. I wouldn't want to live there now because I don't know anyone there. I enjoyed my visit in June. I didn't think I'd ever get back there again." When she returned to Montauk Light in June 2007, she was amused by the amazed reactions of museum visitors who listened to her stories of life at the lighthouse.

"I loved living at Montauk and I especially enjoyed living in the lighthouse," she said in 1996. "There was a definite prestige to being a 'light-house keeper's daughter' and, even now, people are awed by the fact that I had that experience. My husband says that I am still a 'light housekeeper.'"[122]

Looking at the Montauk of 2007 Bucky Bock said:

It used to be a nice little quaint village with all there pretty little houses. How it's overgrown. I will say this—when we first went back (in 1996) my sister went with Bob and me and we stayed overnight at a motel in the center of town. The center of town was like a honky- tonk with all these souvenir shops and motels. And the motel we were in was not cheap! But that's all gone now. At least the buildings that are there now are nice.

We tried to go over to where the old fishing village was and we got lost. So many new roads that never used to be there! Half the population of Montauk lived in the village when I lived here.

As for the Montauk Point Lighthouse she said: "The lighthouse property is very well kept. They're doing a nice job. I'm pleased with that. My father would have been proud."

A congenial Margaret Buckridge Bock reminisces with the author about her years at the Montauk Point Lighthouse at her Westbrook, CT home, July 2007. (Author photo)

In October 1945, only a couple of months after the war ended, Art Dunne concluded his military service and returned to his job where he had worked for many years before as a plant foreman at Bigelow, the renowned carpet manufacturer, in Enfield, Connecticut. The family moved to Chicopee, Massachusetts while continuing to summer in a house at the South Fork Country Club in Amagansett that Art had rented from Mary Gosman during the war. Bigelow closed in Enfield in 1958, and Art began working with Ensign-Bickford. In 1964 the company was taken over by Continental Oil, which planned to close the plant and move it to Oklahoma. It was then that the Dunne family decided to move permanently to Amagansett. Art plied his skills as a carpenter, roofer, plumber, electrician, and mason for many years. He even moved houses, including his own!

Today, Art and Mary live quietly in the same home just off Montauk Highway, sharing a life together that has spanned sixty-six years. The photos displayed in Art's home, and his willingness to share wonderful memories of his years in the service, indicate how proud Art is of his service to his country and the time he spent at Montauk Point.

Arthur and Mary Dunn are pictured at their home in Amagansett, Long Island, in August 2008. Art's memories of life at Montauk Point during World War II underscore the area's strategic importance during the conflict. (Author Photo)

Appendix

The Miller Family
of
Springs and Amagansett, Long Island, New York[123]

The first member of the Montauk Point Lighthouse Miller family of the town of East Hampton was John Miller (died 1663). Born in England, he was among the first settlers of East Hampton, arriving in 1649, a year after the community was founded.

A son, George II, was also born in England, in 1629. He married Hester Conkling, born 1631 in England, in East Hampton in 1650. He died at East Hampton in December 1668 from the kick of a horse. He had five children.

A son of George II, George, was born in East Hampton in 1660 and there married Martha Mulford (born 1665) in 1684. They had six children. He died at East Hampton, October 30, 1712. She died August 21, 1752 in East Hampton.

A son of George, George, was born in 1685 and died in 1770. He married Sarah Conkling (1692-1747) in 1714, and they had ten children. A grandson, Eleazer Miller (1771-1838), did the iron work on the Montauk Lighthouse when it was constructed in 1796.[124]

A son of George, Joseph, was born 1716 and died in 1762. He married Sarah Hedges (1716-1800) in 1739, and they had six children. Sarah was able to speak the language of the Montaukett Indians.

A son of Joseph, Nathan, (1759-1834) lived at East Side, The Springs. He married Mary (Polly) Russell (1770-1845) in 1793 and they had eight children.

A son of Nathan, Jonathan Darrow Miller (1794- February 1, 1861) of Green River, The Springs, married Huldah P. Sherman (1797-1851) of Shelter Island and later married Betsey Baker (1808-1877) of Noyack. With Huldah, Jonathan had eight children.

A son of Jonathan Darrow, **Jonathan Allen Miller** (1834- October 29, 1915), married Margaret Burke (1839-1909) on March 27, 1856. He was the first Miller to be stationed at Montauk Point Lighthouse. He and Margaret had fourteen children:

Huldah Ann (March 12, 1858- May 2, 1864)
Maggie Elma (October 27, 1861- February 17, 1866)
John Ellsworth (May 2, 1863- February 28, 1932)
Charles G (February 1, 1865- 1952)
Mary Elizabeth (October 31, 1866- July 11, 1952)
William Allen (November 19, 1868- August 29, 1869)
Catherine Goodrich (January 2, 1870- ?)
Thomas (June 6, 1872- October 13, 1964)
Wilbur L (August 6, 1873- Dec. 5, 1902); drowned Fort Pond Bay, Montauk
Frank Trenchard (August 6, 1875- died infant)
Florence Bell (October 18, 1876- ?)
Frank Milton (September 25, 1878- June 27, 1944)
Samuel Russell Garfield (June 5, 1881- ?)
Catherine Goodrich (March 2, 1883- May 6, 1937)

One of Jonathan Allen's sons, **John Ellsworth Miller** (May 2, 1863- February 28, 1932), married Mary Alice Ledwith (died June 17, 1930) on October 4, 1887. He was the second Miller to be stationed at Montauk Point. He and Mary had seven children, only one of whom survived to adulthood:

Ethel L (September 12, 1888- died infant)
Florence B (February 21, 1890- died infant)
Jonathan A (February 19, 1891- December 1, 1969)
Frank Sheppard (August 20, 1893- December 31, 1895)
May (May 31, 1896- died infant)
William (October 13, 1897- died infant)
Mary Ledwith (August 18, 1900- March 19, 1903)

The only surviving child, **Jonathan A (Jack) Miller** (February 19, 1891- December 1, 1969), married Maude Irene Finch on November 20, 1911. He was the third Miller to work at Montauk Point Lighthouse. He and Maude had three children:

Eugene Ellsworth (September 14, 1912-1982)
Jonathan Allen (May 29, 1924-)
Richard Daniel (December 19, 1928- December 17, 1950)

Bibliography

Notes on Sources

      The primary sources in publishing this book were interviews conducted with Margaret Buckridge Bock, Jonathan Miller and Arthur M. Dunne. Their first-hand insights into life at Montauk were fascinating, intriguing and exciting.

Books

Keatts, Henry and George Farr. *The Bell Tolls: Shipwrecks and Lighthouses of Eastern Long Island.* Eastport, NY: Fathom Press, 2002.

Osmers, Henry. *On Eagle's Beak.* Denver, CO: Outskirts Press, 2007.

Rattray, Jeannette Edwards. *East Hampton History Including Early Genealogies of Early Families.* Garden City: Country Life Press, 1953.

Rattray, Jeannette Edwards. *Ship Ashore!* New York: Coward, McCann, Inc., 1955.

Newsletters

Beacon. Montauk Historical Society, 1987.

Documents, Letters and Miscellaneous Sources

Bock, Margaret Buckridge. Autobiography for English class, 1935.

Bock, Margaret Buckridge. "Lighthouses: A Nostalgic Era Recalled."

Bock, Margaret Buckridge. Notes on preservation of Montauk Lighthouse, 1967.

Margaret Buckridge Bock Scrapbook. Montauk Point Lighthouse Museum.

National Archives. Record Group 26.

National Archives National Personnel Records Center.

Index

Endnotes

All quotations from Margaret Buckridge Bock, Jonathan Miller, and Arthur Dunne not footnoted in the text were taken from interviews conducted with the author.

Introduction – Montauk/Montauk Point Lighthouse

[1] Letter from the Lighthouse Service to the Commissioner, February 19, 1925. Correspondence of the Bureau of Lighthouses 1911-1939. Box 1004, 50E, File 1546E. National Archives, Record Group 26 (hereafter referred to as NARG 26).

Chapter 1- The Keepers and their Families

[2] Margaret Buckridge Bock. "Lighthouses: A Nostalgic Era Recalled." Presented to Saybrook Colony History Buffs, November 20, 1991.
[3] Letter from Thomas Buckridge to Superintendent of Lighthouses, December 11, 1922. National Archives National Personnel Records Center, St. Louis, MO., (hereafter referred to as NANPRC).
[4] Margaret Buckridge Bock. "Lighthouses: A Nostalgic Era Recalled."
[5] Efficiency Report on John A. Miller age 20 (undated). NANPRC.
[6] Ibid.
[7] Letter from John Miller to the Inspector, September 23, 1913. NANPRC.
* Whale Rock Lighthouse was swept away in the hurricane of September 21, 1938, killing the assistant keeper.
[8] Letter to Eligibles, November 16, 1928. National Archives, National Personnel Records Center (hereafter referred to as NANPRC).
[9] Letter to George Warrington from W.J. Lawton, December 24, 1928. NANPRC.
[10] Letter from George Warrington to Superintendent of Lighthouses, December 26, 1928. NANPRC.
[11] Letter from John E. Miller to Superintendent of Lighthouses, May 1, 1929. NANPRC.

Chapter 2- Life at the Lighthouse

[12] Margaret Buckridge Bock. Autobiography written for English class in 1935.
[13] Margaret Buckridge Bock. "Memories of a Light-Keeper's Daughter."
[14] Ibid.
[15] Margaret Buckridge Bock. "Lighthouses: A Nostalgic Era Recalled."
[16] Margaret Buckridge Bock. "Memories of a Light-Keeper's Daughter."
[17] Margaret Buckridge Bock. "Lighthouses: A Nostalgic Era Recalled."
[18] Jeannette Edwards Rattray. "Montauk Light Built in 1796 Long in Service." *East Hampton Star*. April 28, 1938.
[19] Bock. "Memories of a Light-Keeper's Daughter."
[20] Ibid.
[21] Ibid.
[22] Margaret Buckridge Bock. "Lighthouses: A Nostalgic Era Recalled."
[23] Margaret Buckridge Bock. "Memories of a Light-Keeper's Daughter."
[24] "Century-Old Lighthouse Sight; Popular Mecca for Armies of Tourists." *County Review*. August 17, 1933.
[25] Margaret Buckridge Bock. Autobiography written for English class in 1935.
[26] Margaret Buckridge Bock. "Memories of a Light-Keeper's Daughter."
[27] Ibid.
[28] Ibid.
[29] Ibid.
[30] Ibid.

[31] Ibid.

[32] Ibid.

[33] Ibid.

[34] Margaret Buckridge Bock. Memories of a Light-Keeper's Daughter."

[35] Ibid.

[36] Ibid.

[37] "Kerosene Still Lights Montauk Point Beacon." *East Hampton Star.* May 1933.

[38] Jeannette Edwards Rattray. "Montauk Light Built in 1796 Long in Service." *East Hampton Star.* April 28, 1938.

Chapter 3- Keeping a Good Light

[39] David Behrens. "Keepers of the Lights." *Newsday.* August 6, 1990.

[40] Edward Adolphe. "Montauk Light is Polishing Up to Greet the Summer's Visitors." *New York Times.* May 5, 1937.

[41] "Kerosene Still Lights Montauk Point Beacon." *East Hampton Star.* May, 1933.

[42] Edward Adolphe. "Montauk Light is Polishing Up to Greet the Summer's Visitors." *New York Herald Tribune.* May 5, 1937.

[43] Ibid.

[44] Margaret Buckridge Bock. "Memories of a Light-Keeper's Daughter."

[45] J.T. Yates to Commissioner of Lighthouses, May 28, 1937. Correspondence of the Bureau of Lighthouses 1911-1939. Box 1004, E50, File 1546. NARG 26.

[46] Ibid.

[47] "Washington Does Not Plan Closing Montauk Light." *East Hampton Star.* June 3, 1937.

[48] Margaret Buckridge Bock. "Memories of a Light-Keeper's Daughter."

[49] Report of Damage to Property or Injury to Persons, January 28, 1937. NANPRC.

[50] Letter from Thomas Buckridge to Superintendent of Lighthouse, December 1, 1933. NANPRC.

[51] Letter from J. T. Yates to Thomas Buckridge, December 5, 1933. NANPRC.

[52] Letter from Thomas Buckridge to J. T. Yates, December 6, 1933. NANPRC.

[53] Letter from J. T. Yates to Thomas Buckridge, December 12, 1933. NANPRC.

[54] Letter from Thomas Buckridge to Superintendent of Lighthouses, December 21, 1933. NANPRC.

[55] Margaret Buckridge Bock Scrapbook 1930-1943. Montauk Point Lighthouse Museum.

[56] Ibid.

[57] Ibid.

[58] Ibid.

[59] Letter from J. T. Yates to John A. Miller, 1st Asst. Kpr, June 3, 1927. NANPRC.

[60] Letter from J. T. Yates to John A. Miller, May 26, 1931. NANPRC.

[61] Letter from F. W. Ockenfels, November 30, 1931. NANPRC.

[62] Ibid.

[63] Ibid.

[64] Letter from Superintendent J. T. Yates to John A. Miller, June 6, 1932. NANPRC.

[65] Letter from Superintendent J. T. Yates to Thomas A. Buckridge, June 6, 1932. NANPRC.

[66] Letter from Asst. Supt. F. W. Ockenfels, November 25, 1932. NANPRC.

[67] Letter from Asst. Supt. F. W. Ockenfels, November 25, 1932. NANPRC.

[68] Letter from J. T. Yates to Thomas Buckridge, July 29, 1933. NANPRC.

[69] Letter from Thomas Buckridge to J. T. Yates, August 3, 1933. NANPRC.

[70] Report to Commissioner of Lighthouses, August 14, 1933. NANPRC.

[71] Report of Nomination to new post for Thomas Buckridge, August 14, 1933. NANPRC.

[72] Memorandum to Lighthouse Commissioner George Putnam, September 26, 1933. NANPRC.

[73] Letter from Perry B. Duryea to Daniel C. Roper, September 27, 1933. NANPRC.

[74] Letter from Theodore Monell to Commissioner George Putnam, October 1, 1933. NANPRC.

[75] Letter from Ambrose O'Connell to Daniel C. Roper, October 2, 1933. NANPRC.

[76] Report from W. P. Harman, October 13, 1933. NANPRC.

[77] Letter to Secretary of Commerce from George Putnam, October 19, 1933. NANPRC.

[78] Notice to Thomas Buckridge from Lighthouse Service, November 3, 1933. NANPRC.

[79] Report of Inspection of Light Station, August 17, 1934. Correspondence of the Bureau of Lighthouses 1911-1939. Box 1004, E50, File 1546. NARG 26.

[80] Letter from George Putnam to Thomas Buckridge, August 31, 1934. NANPRC.

[81] Report of Inspection of Light Station, December 6, 1934. Correspondence of the Bureau of Lighthouses 1911-1939. Box 1004, E50, File 1546. NARG 26.

[82] Ibid.

[83] Ibid.

[84] Ibid.

[85] Arthur T. Davis, Commissioner of Health to Bureau of Lighthouses, November 20, 1935. Correspondence of the Bureau of Lighthouses 1911-1939. Box 1004, E 50, File 1546E. NARG 26.

[86] Ibid.

[87] J. T. Yates to Commissioner of Lighthouses, December 14, 1935. Correspondence of the Bureau of Lighthouses 1911-1939. Box 1004, E 50, File 1546E. NARG 26.

[88] R.R. Tinkham to Arthur T. Davis, Commissioner of Health, December 27, 1935. Correspondence of the Bureau of Lighthouses 1911-1939. Box 1004, E 50, File 1546E. NARG 26.

[89] Meier Steinbrink to Commissioner, Bureau of Lighthouses, November 23, 1937. Correspondence of the Bureau of Lighthouses, 1911-1939. Box 1004, E 50, File 1546E. NARG 26.

[90] H. D. King to Meier Steinbrink, December 2, 1937. Correspondence of the Bureau of Lighthouses 1911-1939. Box 1004, E 50, File 1546E. NARG 26.

[91] J. T. Yates to Commissioner of Lighthouses, December 6, 1937. Correspondence of the Bureau of Lighthouses 1911-1939. Box 1004, E 50, File 1546E. NARG 26.

[92] Recommendation as to Aids to Navigation. J. T. Yates to Commissioner of Lighthouses, October 14, 1938. Correspondence of the Bureau of Lighthouses 1911-1939. Box 1004, E 50, File 1546A. NARG 26.

[93] Request to Purchase. C. J. Mancino bid, October 21, 1938. Correspondence of the Bureau of Lighthouses 1911-1939. Box 1004, E 50, File 1546A. NARG 26.

[94] Recommendation as to Aids to Navigation. J. T. Yates to Commissioner of Lighthouses, October 28, 1938. Correspondence of the Bureau of Lighthouses 1911-1939. Box 1004, E 50, File 1546A. NARG 26.

[95] Recommendation as to Aids to Navigation. J. T. Yates to Commissioner of Lighthouses, January 6, 1939. Correspondence of the Bureau of Lighthouses 1911-1939. Box 1004, E 50, File 1546A. NARG 26.

[96] Recommendation as to Aids to Navigation. J. T. Yates to Commissioner of Lighthouses, May 20, 1939. Correspondence of the Bureau of Lighthouses 1911-1939. Box 1004, E 50. File 1546B. NARG 26.

[97] Jeanette Edwards Rattray. Ship Ashore! (New York: Coward, McCann Co, 1955) p.

[98] Thomas Buckridge to Superintendent of Lights. July 14, 1935. NARG 26.

[99] Keatts, Henry, George Farr. "The Bell Tolls: Shipwrecks and Lighthouses of Eastern Long Island." (Eastport, NY: Fathom Press, 2002), p. 121.

[100] Superintendent J. T. Yates to Commissioner of Lighthouses, July 20, 1935. Correspondence of the Bureau of Lighthouses 1911-1939. Box 1004, E50, File 1546. NARG 26.

[101] "Trawler with 40,000 Pounds of Haddock Aground off Montauk." East Hampton Star. November 14, 1935.

[102] Rattray. "Montauk Light Built in 1796 Long in Service."

[103] Margaret Buckridge Bock. "Memories of a Light-Keeper's Daughter."

[104] "Montauk Light Ready for the Long Winter." New York Daily News. October 5, 1939.

[105] Margaret Buckridge Bock Scrapbook. Montauk Point Lighthouse Museum.

[106] J. T. Yates to Commissioner of Lighthouses, April 2, 1937. Correspondence of the Bureau of Lighthouses 1911-1939. Box 1004, E 50, File 1546E. NARG 26.

[107] R. R. Tinkham to Superintendent of Lighthouses, April 16, 1937. Correspondence of the Bureau of Lighthouses 1911-1939. Box 1004, E 50, File 1546E. NARG 26.

[108] J. T. Yates to Commissioner of Lighthouses, April 26, 1937. Correspondence of the Bureau of Lighthouses 1911-1939. Box 1004, E 50, File 1546E. NARG 26.

[109] "Over 10,000 Visitors Climb Historic Montauk Lighthouse." East Hampton Star. August 24, 1939.

[110] Ibid.

[111] Letter from George Warrington to District Coast Guard Officer, Third Naval District, May 15, 1942. NANPRC.

[112] Letter from District Coast Guard Office, Third Naval District, to George Warrington, May 18, 1942. NANPRC.

[113] Enlistment papers for George Warrington dated August 22, 1941. NANPRC.

[114] Margaret Buckridge Bock. "Memories of a Light-Keeper's Daughter."

[115] Jack Graves. *"A Man Who Changed Collars."East Hampton Star.* June 23, 1977.

[116] Ibid.

Chapter 4- End of an Era

[117] Patrick Fenton. "The Keepers of the Light." *Newsday.* June 2, 1996.

[118] Ibid.

[119] "Jonathan Miller, Keeper of Light." *East Hampton Star.* December 4, 1969.

[120] "George Warrington Jr." *East Hampton Star.* February 10, 1955.

[121] Margaret Buckridge Bock. "Lighthouses: A Nostalgic Era Recalled."

[122] Margaret Buckridge Bock. "Memories of a Light-Keeper's Daughter."

Appendix

[123] Jeannette Edwards Rattray, *East Hampton History and Genealogies of Early Families* (Garden City: Country Life Press, 1953), pp. 464,465,468,471,473.

[124] Ibid. p. 463.

CPSIA information can be obtained at www.ICGtesting.com
Printed in the USA
BVOW051626010713

324810BV00002B/14/P